BIG BROAD PRODUCTIONS presents

THE SPEED TWINS

by Maureen Chadwick

First performed at the Riverside Studios, London, on Thursday 29th August 2013

Published by Playdead Press 2013

© Maureen Chadwick 2013

Maureen Chadwick has asserted her rights under the Copyright, Design and Patents Act, 1988, to be identified as the author of this work.

The Gateways Club (1931-1985) © Jill Gardiner 2013

A CIP catalogue record for this book is available from the British Library.

ISBN 978-0-9576792-4-5

Caution

All rights whatsoever in this play are strictly reserved and application for performance should be sought before rehearsals begin to MacFarlane Chard Associates, 33 Percy Street, London W1T 2DF. Email: enquiries@macfarlane-chard.co.uk. No performance may be given unless a license has been obtained.

This book is sold subject to the condition that it shall not by way of trade or otherwise, be lent, resold, hired out, or otherwise circulated without the publisher's prior consent in any form of binding or cover other than that in which it is published and without a similar condition including this condition being imposed on the subsequent purchaser.

Printed by BPUK

Playdead Press
www.playdeadpress.com

THE SPEED TWINS by Maureen Chadwick

Polly Hemingway	Queenie
Amanda Boxer	Ollie/Nurse
Mia Mackie	Shirley/Angelica

Simon Evans	Director
Andrew D Edwards	Designer
Johanna Town	Lighting Designer
Ed Lewis	Sound Designer
Laura Scott	Casting Director
Tim Bray	Associate Lighting Designer
Richard Llewelyn	Company Stage Manager
Patricia Swales	Deputy Stage Manager
Karen Short	Costume Supervisor
Betty Marini	Wigs Supervisor

Kath Gotts	Executive Producer
Douglas McJannet	Producer
Lucy Faulks	Marketing Consultant and Production Support
Simon Gooding and Matt Jones	Production Management Service
Kevin Wilson	Press Representation
Shereden Mathews for DR5	Marketing
Snow Creative	Marketing Design
Kerrie Cronin	Accountancy
Walton & Parkinson Longreach	Insurance

With thanks to:
Archie
Catherine Ashmore
Simon Casson and the team at Duckie
Rebecca Crampton
Maureen Duffy
Georgia Duke
James Duke
Esme Fosbery
Jill Gardiner
Amy Lamé
Daisy Jo Lucas
Maggie Norris
Megan Paran-Rutterford
Greg Richters
Mike Seignot
Alex Souabni
Gina Ware
Robert Workman

Nimax and the Vaudeville Theatre Team
Overthrow Digital
Price Studios
Soho Theatre
Stacey Smith and the team at Riverside Studios

Set built by Cardiff Theatrical Services
Additional sound equipment by Orbital Sound
Additional light equipment provided by Stage Electrics
Cover photograph by Philip Durell

WRITER
Maureen Chadwick

Maureen Chadwick is the creator and writer of a wide range of award-winning, critically acclaimed and controversial shows for both tv and theatre, including single plays, primetime drama series, stage plays and musicals. In 1998, she became one of the co-founders and creative directors of Shed Productions, to write and produce a new wave of entertaining but hard-hitting tv drama series, which included the multiple award-winning, long-running and internationally successful ***Bad Girls***, ***Footballers' Wives*** and ***Waterloo Road***. In 2010, when Shed Media Group had become established as one of the most successful 'super indies' and was taken over by Warner Bros, Maureen left to return to freelance writing with a new slate of projects for tv, theatre and film, the first of which is ***The Speed Twins***, produced through her own company, Big Broad Productions.

Previous tv writing credits include: episodes of ***Angels***, ***Eastenders***, ***Coronation Street***; BBC Screen One single dramas - ***Watch with Mother***, starring Annette Crosbie, ***Two Golden Balls***, starring Kim Cattrall.

Previous theatre writing credits include: the award-nominated musical play ***Joséphine*** (at BAC and on national tour), ***Dust*** (also at BAC), and ***Bad Girls - The Musical***, (at West Yorkshire Playhouse and in the West End).

CAST

AMANDA BOXER Ollie / Nurse

Theatre includes: Lady Cynthia Hayling in *Relative Values* (Theatre Royal Bath), Big Mama in *Cat on a Hot Tin Roof* (West Yorkshire Playhouse), Frieda in *Long Voyage Home* (Old Vic Tunnels), Mary in *The Painter* (The Arcola), Pearl in *Prisoner of Second Avenue* (Vaudeville Theatre), Malka in *Cling to me Like Ivy* (Birmingham Rep), Avril in *Many Roads To Paradise* (Jermyn St. and Finborough), Henrietta Iscariot in *The Last Days Of Judas Iscariot* (Almeida), Carol in *The Pain and the Itch*, Tina in *The Strip* (Royal Court).

Lady Markby in *An Ideal Husband*, Mrs Malaprop in *The Rivals*, (Theatr Clywd). Marie in *Dis-Orientations* (Riverside Studios). Rena in *The Arab Israeli Cookbook* (Gate and Tricycle). Susan in *Angel* (Shadow Factory). Poppy in *A Small Family Business* (West Yorkshire Playhouse). Rena Weeks in *The Destiny of Me* (Finborough). Lady Macbeth in *Macbeth* (Arcola). Mrs Braddock in *The Graduate* (Gielgud). Gittele in *The Yiddish Queen Lear* (Bridewell / Southwark Playhouse). Clytaemnestra in *Iphigenia at Aulis* (Southwark Playhouse). Deborah Harford in *A Touch of the Poet* (Young Vic/Comedy). Martirio in *The House of Bernarda Alba* (Globe). Sue Baylis in *All My Sons*, Portia in *The Merchant of Venice*, Desdemona in *Othello*, Olivia in *Twelfth Night*, Gwendolen in *The Importance of Being Ernest* (The Young Vic). Mrs

Baker in *Come Blow Your Horn*, Mme Pinchard in *The Fall Guy*, Arsinoe in *The Misanthrope*, Marion in *Absurd Person Singular*, Monica in *Present Laughter* (Manchester Royal Exchange). Marion in *Secret Rapture*, Paulina in *Death and the Maiden* (Library Theatre Manchester). Duchess of Berwick in *Lady Windermere's Fan* (Wolsey Ipswich).

Amanda won Best Actress in the 1992 London Fringe Awards for Martha in *Strange Snow*.

Television includes: Fiona Landsley in *Silent Witness* BBC, Nonnie in *Doctors*, Diane in *Casualty*, Dr Clancy in *Bodies 3*. Aunt Ethel in *The Shell Seekers*. Vicky in *Casualty*. Lady Winfield in *Trial and Retribution*. Amanda Trippley in *Chalk*. Clare in *The Ruth Rendell Mysteries - Road Rage*. Stage Manager in *Unnatural Pursuits*. Dorothy in *Inspector Alleyn Mysteries*. Mrs Biggs in *Cider with Rosie*. Rita Marker in *Goodbye My Love*. Victoria Barnett in *In Suspicious Circumstances*.

Films include: Bag Lady in *Malice In Wonderland*. Gail in *Together*. Mrs Sinclair in *Chatroom*. Groom's Mother in *Les Poupées Russes*. Mrs Ryan in *Saving Private Ryan*. Ruth in *Bad Behaviour*.

POLLY HEMINGWAY Queenie

Polly trained at R.A.D.A.

Theatre includes: Lady Macbeth in *Macbeth* and Diaphanta in *The Changeling* (Riverside Studios),

Queen Margaret in ***Richard III*** and Mistress Page in ***The Merry Wives of Windsor*** (Northern Broadsides), Mrs Munning in ***Zack***, Mrs Hardcastle in ***She Stoops to Conquer***, Vita Simmons in ***Harvey*** and best actress award for her performance in ***Road*** (Manchester Royal Exchange), ***I Licked A Slag's Deodorant*** and ***Bazaar & Rummage*** (Royal Court Theatre), Christine in ***Absolute Hell*** (Orange Tree Theatre), Bellamira in ***The Jew of Malta*** (Almeida Theatre), Servant in ***Blood Wedding*** (Young Vic Theatre), Connie in ***Got to be Happy*** (Bush Theatre), Carol in ***All Credit to the Lads*** (Crucible Theatre), ***A Chorus of Disaproval*** (National Theatre), ***Why Me?*** (The Strand Theatre, West End), ***The Homecoming*** (Cambridge Theatre Company), Ivy Benson in ***The Silver Lady*** (Birmingham Rep), Clara Soppit in ***When We Are Married*** and Jean in ***Lucky Sods*** (West Yorkshire Playhouse).

Television includes: Gertrude in ***Wallander*** and Ida Banks in ***DCI Banks*** (Left Bank Pictures), Denise in ***Cracker***, Cynth in ***The Bare Necessities*** and Jean in ***Little Bird*** (Granada), Nelly in ***Wuthering Heights*** (LWT), Gran in ***Johnny Shakespeare***, Mrs Stiles in ***Fingersmith***, Lesley in ***The Locksmith***, May in ***Dalziel And Pascoe***, ***Hetty Wainthorp***, ***Goodnight Sweetheart***, ***Doctors***, ***Casualty*** and ***A Very Polish Practice*** (BBC), ***The Bill***, ***Heartbeat*** and ***Emmerdale*** (ITV), ***Midsomer Murders*** (Bentley Productions), ***Trial and Retribution*** (La Plante Productions) and Gracie Fields in ***Pride of our Alley*** (Yorkshire TV).

Film includes: Mrs Hardcastle in ***She Stoops to Conquer*** (Capriol Films).

MIA MACKIE Shirley/Angelica

Mia trained at Drama Centre. Theatre includes: Nina in ***Ruffled*** Theatre 503, The Duchess in ***The Duchess of Argyll*** Absent season, Royal Opera House, Dreamthinkspeak theatre company, Deirdre in ***The Peddler's Tale***, Edinburgh Festival, Emelda in ***The Never Ever Café***, Clara in ***Rookery Nook*** Menier Chocolate Factory.

Television includes: Jasmine in ***May Day*** Kudos for BBC1, Laura in ***Law & Order: UK*** Kudos for ITV.

Film includes: Poppy in ***The Engagement Party*** directed by Richard Kwietniowski.

COMPANY

SIMON EVANS Director
Simon was Resident Assistant Director at the Donmar Warehouse in 2011, Staff Director at the National Theatre, Creative Associate at the Bush Theatre and Associate Director at the White Bear Theatre. He is Artistic Director of Black and White Rainbow.

Theatre as Director includes: ***Silence of the Sea*** (Donmar Warehouse), ***The Laura Marling Project*** and ***Project Hope/Shawshank Redemption*** (Secret Cinema), ***Thom Pain (based on nothing)*** (Print Room), ***The Rubber Room*** (Old Vic), ***Madness in Valencia*** (Trafalgar Studios), ***Whiff Whaff*** (Theatre Uncut), ***Apple Pie, Hours Till Autumn*** (Riverside Studios), ***Cyrano de Bergerac, The Misanthrope*** (White Bear), ***Us and Them*** (Bush/RR), ***Something Perfect, Disappear, Devolution*** (Theatre503), ***Skyscraper*** (Public, NY), ***ARDEN 2.0*** (Old Vic New Voices), ***Firefly Heartbeat*** (Tristan Bates), ***Singin' in the Rain*** (Cambridge Arts).

Theatre as Associate/Staff/Assistant Director includes: ***The Duchess of Malfi*** (Old Vic), ***Finding Neverland*** (Weinstein Live Entertainment), ***Inadmissible Evidence, Richard II, Anna Christie, Luise Miller, Moonlight, 25th Annual Putnam County Spelling Bee*** (Donmar), ***Men Should Weep*** (NT), ***Like a Fishbone*** (Bush).

Theatre and Film as Writer includes: ***The Waiting*** (SkyArts), ***Who is Rachel?*** (Channel4.com), ***Bait, Somewhere by the Fire*** (Black and White Rainbow).

ANDREW D EDWARDS Designer
Andrew's many theatre credits include ***Quiz Show*** (Traverse Theatre, Edinburgh); ***Donny's Brain*** (Hampstead Theatre); ***Blue Remembered Hills, Playhouse Creatures, Fred's Diner*** (Theatre on the Fly/Chichester Festival Theatre); ***Les Parents Terribles*** (Trafalgar Studios); ***Backbeat*** (West End / Toronto /LA); ***Single Spies, Heroes, Educating Rita*** (Watermill Theatre); ***Birds of a Feather*** (UK Tour); ***A Voyage Around My Father*** (Salisbury Playhouse); ***Measure For Measure*** (Theatre Royal Plymouth / UK Tour); ***Jesus Christ Superstar*** (Madrid / European Tour); ***Shangri-La*** (European Tour); ***No, It Was You*** (Arcola Theatre); ***The Increased Difficulty of Concentration*** (Gate Theatre); ***Broken Voices*** (Tristan Bates Theatre); ***The Smallest Thing*** (The Place); ***This Story of Yours*** (New End Theatre); ***Romeo and Juliet*** (Northampton Theatre); ***The Outsider*** (Etcetera Theatre).

ED LEWIS Sound Designer
Recent theatre includes: ***Cuddles*** (Oval House Theatre), ***Molly Sweeney*** (The Print Room), ***Ignorance*** (Hampstead Theatre), ***Gravity*** (Birmingham Rep Theatre), ***A Midsummer Night's Dream*** (Almeida), ***Thom Pain*** (Print Room), ***On The Rocks, Amongst Friends and Darker Shores*** (Hampstead Theatre),

Slowly, Hurts Given and Received and Apple Pie (Riverside Studios), ***Measure For Measure*** (Cardiff Sherman), ***Emo*** (Bristol Old Vic and Young Vic). Edward studied Music at Oxford University and subsequently trained as a composer and sound designer at the Bournemouth Media School. He works in theatre, film, television and radio. He has recently been nominated for several Off West End Theatre Awards, and films he has recently worked on have won several awards at the LA International Film Festival and Filmstock International Film Festival.

JOHANNA TOWN Lighting Designer
Johanna's West End theatre credits include: ***Fences, What the Butler Saw, Some Like It Hip Hop, Betrayal, Speaking in Tongues, Fat Pig, Hello and Goodbye, Top Girls, Via Dolorosa,*** and ***Beautiful Thing.*** International theatre credits include ***Haunted*** (New York/Royal Exchange/Sydney Opera House); ***Rose*** (National Theatre/Broadway); ***My Name is Rachel Corrie*** (Royal Court/West End/New York); ***Guantanamo*** (New York/Tricycle/West End); ***Arabian Nights, Our Lady of Sligo*** (New York).
She is an Associate Artist for Theatre 503 where recent productions include ***The Life of Stuff*** (Offie nomination for 'Best Lighting Designer'), ***Man in the Middle, The Final Shot and Ship of Fools***. Her many other theatre credits include ***Happy New*** (Trafalgar Studio); ***Joking Apart*** (Salisbury/Nottingham); ***Smack Family Robinson*** (Rose Theatre, Kingston); ***Straight*** (Bush/Sheffield);

Medea, Romeo and Juliet (Headlong/UK Tour); ***Moon on A Rainbow Shawl*** (National); Johanna has also worked extensively at the Royal Court Theatre where her credits include ***Rhinoceros***, ***The Arsonists*** and ***My Child***. She has also lit numerous productions for Out Of Joint including ***Our Country's Good***, ***Bang Bang Bang***, ***Dreams of Violence*** and ***Blue Heart***.

TIM BRAY Associate Lighting Designer
Lighting design includes: ***The Living Room*** (Jermyn Street Theatre), ***The Sound Of Music*** (Kilworth House Theatre), ***Howl's Moving Castle*** (Southwark Playhouse) ***Rinaldo*** (Trinity Laban), ***Fire Island / Carousel*** (Mountview), ***Andersen's English*** (Out of Joint), ***Mixed Up North*** (Out of Joint), ***Albert Herring*** (Trinity), ***The Rivals*** (Southwark Playhouse). Touring extensively as an associate lighting designer and re-lighting productions including: ***Sweeney Todd*** (National Theatre), ***Anna Karenina*** (Shared Experience), ***Oliver Twist*** (Lyric Hammersmith), ***A Midsummer Night's Dream*** (Tim Supple), ***Macbeth*** (National Theatre/OJO), ***Top Girls*** (Oxford Stage Company), ***The Glass Menagerie*** (Theatre Royal Bath), ***The 39 Steps*** (Fiery Angel) ***The Dumb Waiter*** (Oxford Playhouse), ***Highland Fling*** (Matthew Bourne).

BIG BROAD PRODUCTIONS

Big Broad Productions is a creatively-led theatre production company with a strong diversity agenda and a focus on new writing.

www.bigbroad.co.uk
info@bigbroad.co.uk

The Gateways Club (1931-1985)

From 1931 till 1969, the real appeal of the Gateways Club in Chelsea was a well-kept secret, its name passed on by those in the know to those who were desperate to know. Hidden behind a green door, just off the Kings Road in the basement of 239 Bramerton Street, the Gateways began as a Bohemian members club, frequented by artists from the nearby Chelsea Arts Club, who decorated its walls with portraits of regulars. By 1943, when Ted Ware took it over, the Gateways was established as a haven for anyone unconventional; also attracting the friendly and the curious, from Chelsea residents to young West End actors. Its barrel tables, and cut out barrel chairs, were typical of contemporary drinking clubs: its clientele was not.

Among those welcomed down its narrow staircase were artists Augustus John, Jacob Epstein, and Loris Rey (organiser of the Chelsea Arts Balls); and Quentin Crisp, an artist's model, with his hennaed hair and violet shirt. Dylan Thomas and Brendan Behan were thrown out of the Gateways after one drunken afternoon: so, on separate occasions, were Diana Dors and Kenneth Williams. Local resident Joan Collins was once spotted there with her father in the 1950s, when it was also frequented by Clement Freud, proprietor of the Royal Court Theatre, actress Jacqueline Mackenzie (later reincarnated as lesbian activist Jackie Forster), and TV personality Nancy Spain. Among the ethnically diverse clientele, black musicians were welcomed: whenever Chester Harriott played jazz piano there, he was surrounded by crowds of women, singing lustily. By the early 1960s, the jukebox had replaced the piano, and the fashionably dressed dropped in from the Kings Road. Dusty Springfield was regularly seen at the Gateways, off duty, with short ginger hair and no wig, in dark tight trousers and a shirt, accompanied by a friend in gaily coloured skirts.

Mingling with them all were smartly dressed couples, often mistaken for men and women; who, in fact, were women in men's suits and their girlfriends in frocks, lipstick and heels. In this butch-femme role-playing scene, women identified possible partners by their sexily different style of dress, and behaviour. Butches often adopted male names, and would ask femmes to dance. While femmes could pass as straight, some butches, unable or unwilling to hide their identity, worked in "male" jobs like chauffeuring, or were self-employed. Others were accepted as "characters" at work if they replaced their trousers with a skirt, tweed or not. For many, "the Gates" was the one place they could be themselves: like Dusty, Britain's leading woman singer, they felt obliged to hide their attraction to women elsewhere. Some couples, even before unisex fashion arrived in the mid-1960s, insisted on dressing similarly - usually in trousers - but often signalled, by accessories or footwear, who was more butch or femme. Sexuality frequently reflected roles, but might be more fluid - some were "butch on the streets, femme between the sheets" or "versatile" (able to swop roles).

The Gateways became increasingly gay under Ted Ware. When one man was hassling a couple at the bar, Ted sided with the women and had him ejected, announcing that he would have a club full of lesbians if he wanted. Word got round and he had his wish. Nowhere else in London could gay women be sure of meeting every night of the week. The Gateways' appeal grew when Ted married Gina, a glamorous young actress in 1953, and especially after 1958, when Smithy, a boyish American airforce-woman, came to work behind the bar and live with the Wares and their daughter. Rumours that Gina and Smithy were a couple were always denied by them, but added to the attraction of the club as Ted, who turned 60 in 1958, increasingly left them to run it.

For a woman who recognised that she was attracted to women, it was a challenge to find this world. There was plenty in the press about gay men, and their then illegal sex life, decriminalised (partially) only in 1967. But lesbianism, though legal, remained relatively invisible. More than one young woman, in love with another girl, had no word for it, so consulted her GP on whether she was turning into a boy. Many assumed, or hoped, that they would grow out of such feelings and married, only to realise their mistake later. If a woman was discovered to be gay, it carried the same risks as for a man - losing her job, losing her home, possible rejection by family and friends. The risk of divorce could hit such women particularly hard, as female earnings were half those of men, and loss of children was certain. Some lived a double life. Others did not dare.

Before the 1970s, lesbian venues did not advertise: women found the Gateways by word of mouth. If you knew no lesbians, that was difficult. Sometimes a butch woman would be spotted by another, or two women visibly in love, believing they were the only ones in the world, were enlightened by a sympathetic gay man or heterosexual. Bold women asked a London taxi driver where lesbians went and were whisked to the Gateways. Some, pressed into "treatment", found out from their psychiatrist or from other patients. The one lesbian magazine, *Arena 3*, was mainly available by mail order, and not widely known. There were spasmodic mainstream publications, press articles and TV documentaries about gay women between 1964 and 1968, notably Maureen Duffy's 1966 best-selling novel *The Microcosm*, set around the Gateways (renamed the House of Shades), but none of these gave its exact location, for fear of attracting violence to members in the street.

All this changed in March 1969, when the Gateways burst across the big screen in a Hollywood movie, *The Killing of Sister George*. In a ten-minute fancy dress party scene, Susannah York (Childie) and Beryl Reid (George), play a lesbian couple dressed as Stan Laurel and Oliver Hardy (Ollie) in suits, ties and bowler hats. Their comic dance routine is applauded by 80 ordinary club members, who then smooch cheek to cheek. Gina greets new arrivals in her sparkly black dress; Smithy serves behind the bar. When Coral Browne arrives, playing George's boss, Mrs

Croft, she seems stunned by the Gateways (though later in the film she seduces Childie).

The club's name, address and phone number were announced on screen, much to its proprietors' horror. The film's director, Robert Aldrich, had not consulted them, assuming they would welcome the resulting surge in membership. Nor had he mentioned the film's sex scene (which generated front page publicity); or sadism, when George forces her girlfriend to eat her cigar butt. Gina was mortified by this negative portrayal, so unlike the relationships of women she knew, and regretted her suggestion that club members be employed as extras, feeling that they and the Gateways had been exploited.

However, the filming created a huge buzz at the time. Beryl Reid and Susannah York were taken to the club to experience the atmosphere. One butch grasped the opportunity to teach Susannah to dance the "Gateways grind", cheek to cheek, thigh to thigh, while Beryl signed autographs and encouraged members to join in the filming. Urged to wear fancy dress, those who wanted to hide could, with one woman disguised as Batman all week. Few wore sunglasses: most came as themselves. Some assumed the film would attract little attention; others were already open with those who mattered.

One butch, barred from the club by Gina, was lingering wistfully outside, when the film crew recruited her. Unbarred for the filming, she winked and blew a kiss to a femme who fancied her, which was edited in to appear to be directed at Coral Browne. Two doorkeepers, deep in conversation on the stairs, were told not to move, so Mrs Croft has to push past: for courteous butches this went against the grain. Susannah York recalled a lot of laughs and everyone enjoying themselves. Everyone found her and Beryl Reid very friendly, as they sat in the breaks with groups of Gateways members, asking with interest about their lives. Beryl would tell them they were all lovely: when positive remarks about lesbians were rare, this was a real boost. Coral Browne remained pleasant but reserved, preparing for her part by staying in her dressing room. After the filming, a party was thrown at the club for Beryl Reid's birthday, where members presented her with flowers and brandy.

Once the "LESBIAN FILM!" headlines died down, the Gateways Club was firmly established as the place any gay woman could go, and until it closed in 1985, was where many went first, even though other venues emerged in the greater openness of the 1970s. While gay liberation, launched by the Stonewall riots of June 1969, steadily raised awareness, it was Gateways Club members who "came out" earlier, before the term was known to them, to roars of approval from members of cinema audiences, who looking around them, suddenly realised that they were not alone.

Jill Gardiner, author of *From the closet to the screen: women at the Gateways Club 1945-1985* (Pandora Press)

CHARACTERS

Queenie
Ollie
Shirley
Nurse
Angelica

NB The actor playing Shirley also plays Angelica. The actor playing Ollie also plays the Nurse.

Author's Thanks
With special thanks to April de Angelis, Amanda Barrie, Deborah, Jill Gardiner and Maggie Norris.

The text went to press before the end of rehearsals and so may differ slightly from the play as performed.

THE SPEED TWINS

ACT ONE

Out of the darkness we hear a distorted soundscape of bleeps, buzzers, heartbeats and laboured breathing. This culminates in a single sustained hum, which is suddenly cut off.

QUEENIE appears in a separate space, hands over her eyes, as if stiff with fear of what the darkness holds.

She is an old woman dressed as a 1960s beauty queen, with a 'Miss United Kingdom' sash and a little coronet atop her lustrous dark wig.

Dusty Springfield starts to sing 'I Only Want To Be With You' and atmospheric lighting fades up to reveal a basement club.

QUEENIE lowers her hands and surveys her new surroundings.

There's a bar with shelves of bottles and optics, with mirror-glass behind and a couple of bar stools in front. To one side of the bar is a door with a 'toilet roll' sign. Incorporated in the decor is a faded mural with peeling portraits of the club's former habituées amidst a collage of playing cards and fragments of mirrors.

There's a banquette in a corner, a table and stools made out of beer barrels down stage, and a jukebox to one side of the small dance floor.

The club is otherwise empty, except for one character sitting slumped at the bar - OLLIE. She is an old woman dressed as Oliver Hardy, bowler hat atop a Beryl Reid mop.

The music fades into the background as QUEENIE takes stock and galvanises.

QUEENIE Bit of a dump, isn't it?

She espies the figure slumped over the bar.

     That's my companion for the evening, is it? I'll go and mingle, then.

She makes her way towards OLLIE.

     Hello? May I disturb you?

No response. QUEENIE looks around.

     If nobody else is going to come to my rescue...

She taps OLLIE on the shoulder.

     Excuse me, hello?

OLLIE jolts awake.

OLLIE Well-halle-finally-bloody-lujah! Company! A glamour-puss!

She raises her glass and falls off her bar stool.

     Whoops! Down she goes. *(Snorts)* Over-excited. Get a grip. *(Picks herself up, with exaggerated effort)* A-one and a-two. And up she comes. *(Doffs bowler and bows)* Boop-a-do.

QUEENIE's slightly disconcerted but presses on.

QUEENIE   May we be introduced?

OLLIE   We certainly may. *(Extending her hand)* Call me Ollie.

QUEENIE   *(Extending her hand)* I'm – Queenie.

OLLIE   Delighted to meet you, Queenie.

OLLIE gives her hand a vigorous shake, squints at her face.

           Did we hook up before, on some such night? Have to ask, memory's worse than my eyesight.

QUEENIE   I'm sure we can only be meeting as strangers. I'm a complete newcomer to this place.

OLLIE   Must be soul-mates of a sort, eh? *(Snorts)* Look a right pair, don't we? Here, let me prepare you a throne.

She whips out a hanky from her breast pocket to make great show of polishing the seat of a bar stool.

QUEENIE   Not exactly swarming with life here, is it?

OLLIE   *(Chortles)* You could say that. Must be the early birds. *(Bows)* There you are, ma'am!

QUEENIE   Thank you, kind sir.

She sits on the bar stool, legs demurely crossed. OLLIE refolds the hanky into her breast pocket.

OLLIE   Fancy dress always helped oil the wheels, eh? Christ knows how they sort the boys from the girls nowadays, all mix 'n' match lippy and long hair. Bloody *is* another planet.

QUEENIE   I wouldn't know what you're talking about.

OLLIE   Just you relax and let me take the lead, eh? *(Goes behind the bar)* So - what's your medicine?

QUEENIE   I have to take whatever I'm given now, don't I?

OLLIE   Okey-dokes. If you carry on like this we'll get on a treat. *(Starts to fix drinks)* 'Honesty' bar. Got to laugh, eh?

QUEENIE   I have to accept that I'm dying, apparently.

OLLIE   Uh-huh?

QUEENIE   I've tried to keep a sense of humour. But I do have flashes of rage.

OLLIE   Oh dear. Better watch out for them, then.

QUEENIE   Melanoma. My punishment for being a sun-worshipper. The least of my sins, I'm sure.

OLLIE   We all have to go somehow. Boop-a-do.

QUEENIE   I just can't face it, to be frank. I'm still hoping for a miracle.

OLLIE   Uh-huh?

QUEENIE   You don't believe in miracles, then?

OLLIE   Me? Don't ask, love. I'm a mystery to myself now.

QUEENIE   I've already survived eighteen months beyond my last no-hope prognosis. I went back to Spain and lay on the beach.

OLLIE   Defiant to the last, eh?

QUEENIE   I'm just not ready to give up. Why should I? In my mind I'm perfectly capable.

OLLIE   No doubt about that.

QUEENIE   And one should rage, at my age. I play bridge with women in their eighties - nineties - who've survived multiple life-threatening setbacks - perfectly capable. You don't just give up and go. Well, not in my book.

OLLIE   You're a fighter all right.

QUEENIE   All my life. I've had to be.

OLLIE   Given that you're here, though, dear - don't you think you might have to accept that you've already went?

QUEENIE falters.

	Where do you think you are, eh? In the patients' lounge?
QUEENIE	All I remember is walking to the end of the corridor. I just wanted to be anywhere rather than stay in that bed.
OLLIE	*(Chuckles)* You've arrived now, Queenie, love. Come on, work it out. Our very own place, decked out like the dear old Gateways Club? That's forever Saturday night, Sunday morning? Dusty on the jukebox? Free booze on tap? *(QUEENIE's blank)* You're in Dyke Heaven, darling!
QUEENIE	What?
OLLIE	Where else?

QUEENIE starts to panic.

QUEENIE	I need my nurse.
OLLIE	Oh come on Queenie, we're past all that.
QUEENIE	I want my nurse. *(Calls out)* Where's my nurse!

She tries to escape.

	Nursie!
OLLIE	You can't go back, you soft nelly.
QUEENIE	Help me! I need help!

OLLIE   *(Serving drinks)* Just help yourself to a stiff drink and thank The Powers That Be we can still get slaughtered.

QUEENIE pulls herself up.

QUEENIE   No - no - *(Laughs)* This can't be happening. It's ridiculous. I'm not here. I'm delusional.

OLLIE   Neck this Scotch, you'll be tops.

QUEENIE   This is the morphine, this is what it does. Just now - I remember - I thought poor Tufty was about to be run over by a bus.

OLLIE   Tufty? Did I know a Tufty?

QUEENIE   Tufty my dog. It was so vivid. I remember I cried out: 'Look out for Tufty!' But there he was, safe in his basket.

OLLIE   Sweet.

QUEENIE   Just the morphine…

OLLIE   My last words as I recall were 'Fuck Princess Margaret'. Which I think I possibly did once. In Cannes or somewhere? Antibes? Anyway, one of us chums had the pleasure, wherever it was, oh yes. One of our star conquests, wasn't she, Princess Marge? Could be powdering her nose in the lavs as we speak.

QUEENIE sinks to her knees in desperate prayer.

QUEENIE	Hail Mary full of Grace -
OLLIE	Oh no / don't do that -
QUEENIE	The Lord is with thee -
OLLIE	It's against the rules -
QUEENIE	Blessed art thou among women -
OLLIE	You really don't / want to provoke -
QUEENIE	And blessed is the fruit of thy womb Jesus…

The lights have dimmed right down and there's an ominous bass rumble, getting louder.

OLLIE   I told you, look out -

She dives for cover behind the bar.

QUEENIE   Holy Mary Mother of God pray for us sinners now and at the hour of our death / Amen -

Before QUEENIE can finish, there's a resounding whiplash CRACK. And one of the optics explodes, spectacularly.

QUEENIE reels.

The lighting state reverts and OLLIE reappears, with a sigh.

OLLIE   Well that's the Scotch gone. You get the message now, Queenie? Even had the same daft urge myself on arrival. Most bizarre. Born again atheist suddenly reciting the Lord's Prayer? Slam, bang, wallop - magnum of vintage Krug blasted to buggery. So please don't go there again, 'cos we don't know how long these precious stocks have got to last us, do we? Or how many other chums are coming for last orders.

QUEENIE   This is frightening me.

OLLIE brings her drink.

OLLIE   Go on, knock it right back. You need a stiffener. Down the hatch.

QUEENIE downs the drink. OLLIE waits to see if it takes effect. QUEENIE seems to calm, then suddenly starts to hyperventilate.

QUEENIE   Please - just hold my hand.

OLLIE   Okey-dokes.

She holds QUEENIE's hand.

Calm down. Deep breaths. Nice and slow.

QUEENIE   Are you holding it?

OLLIE   Yep, I'm right here, holding your hand. And a very shapely and beautifully manicured hand it is indeed.

She kisses it. QUEENIE takes deep slow breaths and begins to calm right down, to the point of trance.

QUEENIE   I had my toes done as well.

OLLIE   Very saucy.

QUEENIE   I thought it was important, not to let myself go.

OLLIE   Absolutely. You're a stunner.

Blows on QUEENIE's hand and rubs it.

QUEENIE   Don't leave me, will you?

OLLIE   No chance.

QUEENIE   Promise me.

OLLIE   Brownie's honour. Though I might have to move about a bit.

QUEENIE's stilled, eyes shut.

           How do you feel now?

QUEENIE   I can't feel anything. I'm completely numb.

OLLIE   Soon catch up with yourself. Have a sit down, I'll get the next round in.

She leads trance-like QUEENIE to sit on a cushioned beer barrel, then goes back behind the bar to fix drinks.

QUEENIE   My mind's all a-jumble. So many questions.

OLLIE   Yep. Then they all boil down to 'What happens next?'

QUEENIE   Do you know the answer?

OLLIE   Nup. Just going with the flow and staying hopeful.

QUEENIE   I think my faith is being tested.

OLLIE   Just don't reach for the rosary again.

QUEENIE   Of course I can't believe you're right. About where we are. It's not possible.

OLLIE   What's your explanation, then?

QUEENIE   There is only one I could accept. If I have to accept my own death...

She wavers, uncertain.

OLLIE   *(Out-of-sight behind bar)* I'm listening...

QUEENIE   Then we must be in some form of Purgatory. To give us a chance to repent our remaining sins. *(A snort from OLLIE)* Though I don't understand how *you* could be in a state of grace...

OLLIE   *(Bringing drinks to the table)* Don't you worry about me? I'm finding all the joys I need right here. Look!

She beams as she produces a large cigar.

           My favourite, Romeo and Juliet. Must have some matches on me somewhere.

She pats her pockets. QUEENIE snaps to attention.

QUEENIE   You can't *smoke*!

OLLIE brandishes a box of matches.

OLLIE   Oh yes I can!

QUEENIE	You're not allowed. It's against the law.
OLLIE	*(Snorts)* No such loopy law here.
QUEENIE	I can't bear cigar smoke. I hate it. I never want to smell it again, ever. I mean it.
OLLIE	Oh bloody hell.
QUEENIE	It's a filthy habit. Just say 'No'!
OLLIE	Now you're bringing out the rebel in me.
QUEENIE	I don't know how you can even think of putting that foul thing in your mouth. The very sight of it revolts me.
OLLIE	You've never smoked, then, I take it?
QUEENIE	No, I have not.
OLLIE	Well here's your chance, Queenie. You can have your first puff in the certain knowledge that it really won't kill you.
QUEENIE	Are you listening to me at all? I told you I hate the smell of it. I hate the very thought of it. I'm completely and utterly intolerant of it.
OLLIE	I think I'm picking up a hint of that rage you warned me about.
QUEENIE	I have a right to insist you don't do it in my presence.

OLLIE	Okey-dokes… Here's what. Compromise. I'll go puff it over here. You look away and ignore me.
QUEENIE	No! I'll know you're doing it and I insist that you don't.
OLLIE	Look, I'm not asking you to eat the bloody butt. You'll hardly catch a whiff if you keep your distance. Oh come on, Queenie, got to show a bit of give and take.

She moves aside. QUEENIE dashes to the bar and grabs a soda siphon.

QUEENIE	If you set light to that thing, I shall extinguish it.
OLLIE	When you used to go to gay clubs, were you wearing a police uniform?
QUEENIE	Please throw that cigar away. Now!
OLLIE	I can see you in black stockings, being forceful…
QUEENIE	For the last time -

OLLIE puts the cigar in her mouth and strikes a match. And QUEENIE lets fly with the soda stream. OLLIE doesn't react, she just droops, soggy cigar still in her mouth.

You made me do that.

OLLIE is silent and still.

> I told you what would happen. It's your own fault.

OLLIE silently and precisely replaces the box of matches in her trouser pocket, puts the cigar in her inside breast pocket, removes the handkerchief from her outer breast pocket, shakes it out and dabs herself down.

QUEENIE gears herself up for a declaration.

> I understand perfectly now. I'm not like *you*. I'm not one of your 'chums'. The only possible reason I'm here is to try and save your soul.

OLLIE rings out her hankie and refolds it into her breast pocket.

> I know you people resent being challenged - it must be difficult to reject the unhealthy habits of a lifetime, trying to convince yourself they're defensible. But you know why they provoke such revulsion - smoking, sexual perversion. They give off the bad odour of antisocial self-indulgence.

OLLIE walks silently to the table and proceeds to down one of the drinks.

> It's no excuse to cite deviant behaviour in the animal kingdom. As if Nature has any bearing on morality! The expression of human desire is subject to will power. You

just have to decide to change your behaviour to conform with the norm.

OLLIE downs the other drink.

> Well aren't you even going to argue with me?

OLLIE   Nup. I'm going to the lav to avail myself of the hot air dryer - or a steamy clinch with Princess Marge, whichever comes first.

QUEENIE   You're just ducking the issue. Now I've spelt it out.

OLLIE   Boop-a-do.

QUEENIE   And as if there'd be a need for lavatories in the afterlife - well that proves it's all a nonsense.

OLLIE turns to give her an old-fashioned look.

OLLIE   Proves what goes in still has to come out, Queenie. Think about it.

She exits through the door with the 'toilet roll' sign. QUEENIE's left on her own as the lights dim down and a low humming noise starts up. QUEENIE looks up and around, fearful again.

QUEENIE   How can this be? It can't…

The fragments of mirror glass glint, flickering light on the faces in the mural. QUEENIE catches their eyes and recoils.

> As if I would be seen dead in a place like this. I must be drugged... They've upped my dose. Trying to 'ease me off'.

The humming noise blasts up in volume, like a hot air dryer from Hell. QUEENIE shouts upwards.

> I don't want to be *managed*! I told you - just give me back my pain and let me go home!

The hot air dryer suddenly cuts out and the lighting state plunges into darkness. QUEENIE's confounded.

> What's going on now?

Silence and darkness.

> Is this a power cut or what?

Darkness and silence.

> You can't leave me alone - in the dark?

The lights flicker.

> I have to be strong, have faith...

The lights brighten as the loo door opens and OLLIE returns.

OLLIE Sadly no sign of Princess Marge. But I found an old gem scratched on the wall: 'My mother made me a lesbian' - 'If I gave her the wool would she make me one, too?'

QUEENIE gives her a frozen stare in response. OLLIE doffs her bowler and bows.

> Boo-boom?

QUEENIE's rigid. OLLIE heaves a sigh and slumps, then shakes herself back up with a shrug.

>Okay grumpy chops, I'll talk to myself.

She heads behind the bar and plays barman and customer.

>*(Barman)* What's your pleasure, sir? *(Customer)* I think a large G & T would hit the spot. *(Barman)* Shall I make that a treble? Ice and lemon? *(Customer)* Oh go on, twist my arm, you devil.

She casts an eye at QUEENIE as she mixes the drink.

>Anything for you, your Royal Highness? While I'm here to serve.

QUEENIE snaps back into hostile mode.

QUEENIE   Actually, you do remind me of someone. Someone I don't like in the least.

OLLIE   Ditto, darling.

QUEENIE   Over-familiar endearments being one of your many repellent traits.

OLLIE   Oh give it up, Queenie, for crying out. Why can't you just try and be a chum? You bloody need one, don't you?

QUEENIE turns her back again. OLLIE despairs of her.

>Well I bloody boop-a-do.

She takes her drink over to the jukebox and fishes in her pocket for change.

>					Let's have another golden oldie - and hope there's one on her way.

QUEENIE			Your only hope here is *me*.

OLLIE ignores, putting coins in the machine and pressing buttons. QUEENIE takes herself to the bar.

>					I'm going to mix my own medicine. Wait for *you* to face some hard facts.

The jukebox lights up and Helen Shapiro starts to sing 'Walkin' Back To Happiness'. OLLIE swigs and sings along. QUEENIE busies herself with the optics.

Then SHIRLEY appears. She's a vivacious young woman in her early twenties, wearing a 1960s frock and blond beehive, with one leg in an old-fashioned calliper.

The music fades into the background as she makes her way on to the dance floor, looking around in gleeful amazement.

SHIRLEY			Oh my gosh!

QUEENIE freezes at the sight of her.

>					Why, it's just like that club - in the film - 'The Killing of Sister George'...

OLLIE			Well-halle-finally-bloody-lujah!

She adjusts her tie and goes to greet, doffing her bowler.

>					Greetings, m'dear! Whoever you are you're most welcome.

SHIRLEY			I'm Shirley. Are you - you're not Beryl Reid?

OLLIE   Ollie. Just call me Ollie.

SHIRLEY   *(Doing a Stan Laurel)* Okay, Ollie.

OLLIE   And skulking behind the bar over there is our Queenie.

SHIRLEY   *(Waves)* Hello, Queenie!

OLLIE   Queenie, this is Shirley. Going to say hello?

QUEENIE can't speak. She turns away, knocks back her drink and pours another, very rattled.

                (To SHIRLEY) Think you've queered her pitch.

SHIRLEY's absorbed by her surroundings.

SHIRLEY   Gosh, is this - can it be - have I really gone to my very own Heaven?

OLLIE   Dyke Heaven, dearie. Where else?

SHIRLEY's hands go to her face in delighted wonderment.

SHIRLEY   Oh my! I think I'm going to cry.

OLLIE   Just don't express yourself in prayer.

SHIRLEY   Oh this is totally against my religion. That's why I'm so happy. It's my dream come true!

OLLIE   Certainly looking more dreamy now you've joined us. Let me fix you a drink. We get to do that, too. What a hoot, eh? What will you have?

SHIRLEY   I'll have a sherry, please.

OLLIE goes behind the bar.

OLLIE   'Scuse me, Queenie.

QUEENIE darts out of her way, gulping her drink.

QUEENIE   This isn't happening.

OLLIE   Oh yes it is.

SHIRLEY   Where's everyone else got to, though? Shouldn't it be absolutely packed?

OLLIE   The Gates was never easy to find.

SHIRLEY   I didn't know it really existed till after it closed down.

OLLIE   Must be legions of dead old dykes roaming around the cosmos trying to find the way in.

SHIRLEY   I was the lucky one, then.

OLLIE   Dead lucky, eh?

SHIRLEY   Oh - Right! Yes, dead lucky!

She laughs, self-consciously. OLLIE chortles as she fixes drinks.

OLLIE   D'you remember old Smithy in the film? Behind the bar? *(American accent)* Yeah, sherry coming up. *(Own voice)* Stiff as a bloody board.

SHIRLEY	I remember everything about that film. It was all I had to prove I wasn't the only one in the world.

OLLIE serves up the drinks.

OLLIE	Well you've come home now, eh? Cheers!
SHIRLEY	Cheers!
OLLIE	God help you, though, if that hideous sex scene was your introduction. Still gives me the heebie-jeebies.
SHIRLEY	I was grateful for anything then.
OLLIE	The smouldering Coral Browne with her gymnastic eyebrows, sitting bolt upright and fully dressed beside the limp Susannah York, twiddling her nipple like she's tuning a bloody radio? *(Mimics à la Coral Browne, with one hand behind her back, the other tweaking an imaginary nipple, eyebrows arching maniacally)* No wonder folk marvelled how lesbians did it.

She snorts and SHIRLEY giggles. And QUEENIE erupts.

QUEENIE	She isn't one of *you*, you disgusting old drunk. She's just here to haunt *me*.
OLLIE	Beg your pardon?
QUEENIE	Well it won't work, Shirley. You can follow me to the ends of the earth and

                    beyond but you'll still be wasting your
                    time.

SHIRLEY looks at her, perplexed.

OLLIE   *(To SHIRLEY)* Do you two know each
                other of old?

SHIRLEY   I think there's some mistake.

QUEENIE   Yes there is and you're making it. So just
                give up and leave me alone!

SHIRLEY   I don't know what she means. Why is she
                so angry?

OLLIE   Would you mind explaining what you
                mean, Queenie? We're both a bit
                perplexed.

QUEENIE   Oh this is so devilish! Oh the cunning
                tricks and traps… *(To OLLIE)* Don't you
                understand? She's only here because I
                thought of her.

She turns away from them, holding her hands over her ears and droning 'God Save The Queen'.

SHIRLEY   Is she all right?

OLLIE   She had other plans for me and her. Must
                say, though, you are miraculously well
                preserved for one of our vintage.

SHIRLEY   Am I?

OLLIE	You don't know? Take a look at yourself in the mirror.

She directs her to stand in front of the mirror behind the bar. SHIRLEY's amazed, delighted.

SHIRLEY	Oh my gosh! I've gone back fifty years. What did we use to look like?
OLLIE	It's delightful to be reminded.
SHIRLEY	I can't believe it. I hardly recognise myself.
OLLIE	Reckon you're going to liven us all up. Even a rotten old corpse like you, eh Queenie?
QUEENIE	Not listening, go away.
OLLIE	*(To SHIRLEY)* Well sod her. You've certainly perked me up no end.

But SHIRLEY's crestfallen, looking down at her calliper.

SHIRLEY	Still got this gammy old leg on me, though.

QUEENIE drones.

> At least it doesn't hurt anymore. But I never would've worn this frock after the accident. I hated people looking at me being a cripple.

QUEENIE drones louder as SHIRLEY stares at herself.

OLLIE   *(Hissing)* Queenie! Will you clam up? The poor girl's trying to get her bearings.

QUEENIE   *(Hissing back)* I told you, she's a phantom. Don't believe in her, block her out.

OLLIE   I'll block you out / if you don't -

SHIRLEY   Oh dear...

She turns away from the mirror, emotional.

        I always knew that was the day I really died. Inside. When I really *felt* I'd lost my life, you know? When your whole world's suddenly destroyed, all your hopes and dreams smashed to bits... But I couldn't tell anyone else. I had to pretend it was just my leg.

OLLIE   Aw pet -

SHIRLEY   We had to pretend so much in those days, didn't we?

OLLIE   Don't upset yourself. We're not here to be miserable.

SHIRLEY chokes back a sob.

SHIRLEY   Sorry -

OLLIE   Come and have a cuddle. Here -

She opens her arms and QUEENIE snaps.

QUEENIE   Oh spare me! *(To OLLIE)* Are you even more stupid than you look? Don't you know how the Devil works? The oh so sweet and subtle seduction? Flaunting that thing on her leg, asking for pity! Well don't go flattering yourself it's *your* saggy bosom she wants to worm into.

SHIRLEY   *(To OLLIE)* Why is she saying these things?

OLLIE   *(To QUEENIE)* Bet they had to bury you under concrete, you poisonous old bag.

QUEENIE   That accident was a judgement. She didn't die, she was saved!

The lights dim down fast.

OLLIE   Oh shit.

QUEENIE   *(Pulling herself up)* Oh why am I doing this to myself?

OLLIE   Just stop provoking The Powers That Be.

QUEENIE   'The Powers That Be'! Another figment.

The deep bass rumble starts up, increasing in volume. SHIRLEY looks around in alarm.

OLLIE   Queenie!

QUEENIE   As if I've anything to atone for -

OLLIE   You've been warned -

QUEENIE   After all my struggles, all my sacrifices -

OLLIE   Just think of our precious booze!

QUEENIE   I will not be tempted! I will not have doubts!

OLLIE   Queenie, shut the fuck up now or you're going to regret this.

More volume - the rumble sounding more like the roar of a monstrous motorbike.

SHIRLEY   What's happening?

OLLIE   *(Grabbing SHIRLEY)* Take cover!

She pulls SHIRLEY to safety as QUEENIE shouts.

QUEENIE   I will not be sorry!

There's a hideous screeching sound, followed by an echoing metallic CRASH.

SHIRLEY screams.

The lighting state reverts to reveal a metal grille locked down in front of the rows of bottles and optics.

OLLIE looks up from her hiding place, aghast.

OLLIE   Oh no…

SHIRLEY looks up with her hands over her eyes.

SHIRLEY   What's happened?

OLLIE investigates behind the bar.

OLLIE   Oh no, oh please no -

SHIRLEY   Is it really bad?

OLLIE   Look at it! We've lost everything.

SHIRLEY   Oh please don't say that. I can't bear things to be final.

OLLIE turns on QUEENIE, who stands stock still, facing out front, as if the crash sfx have transported her elsewhere.

OLLIE   You see what you've done? You see what you've *done* to us?

QUEENIE replies as if to somebody else.

QUEENIE   Don't be sad.

OLLIE   It's worse than tragic!

QUEENIE   We must count our blessings and be grateful.

OLLIE   *Grateful?*

And SHIRLEY takes her hands from her eyes to stare at QUEENIE, struck, as if a veil is being lifted.

QUEENIE   You know it's all for the best.

OLLIE   Are you stark raving nuts?

QUEENIE   It will be, you'll see. One day, you'll see.

OLLIE   I don't want to see another second now. I'd rather be stone cold dead and done for.

QUEENIE   No, you don't really mean that. You wait. You'll have everything to live for, we both will. Husbands, children -

OLLIE — I don't want a husband and bloody kids, you lunatic! I want a bloody G & T!

QUEENIE jolts out of her private reverie, disorientated.

QUEENIE — Who are you? Where am I?

SHIRLEY goes to grab hold of QUEENIE's hands.

SHIRLEY — Look into my eyes. Look at me…

QUEENIE briefly looks at SHIRLEY, then jolts away. SHIRLEY's staggered.

Oh my…

QUEENIE clamps her hands to her head, swaying.

Why are you still so scared?

OLLIE — Oh don't try and work her out. We've just got to make her plead for forgiveness so they'll give us back our booze.

SHIRLEY — She can't forgive herself.

OLLIE — To hell with that. *(To QUEENIE)* Just say you're sorry to the Powers That Be.

QUEENIE — I need a priest.

OLLIE — You don't need a bloody priest! Just beg for mercy.

QUEENIE sinks to her knees in desperate prayer.

QUEENIE — Bless me Father / for I have sinned -

OLLIE — Not like that!

Yanks her up.

SHIRLEY   Please - can I speak to her? On my own?

OLLIE   Oh help yourself. I've had it.

OLLIE throws up her hands and withdraws.

SHIRLEY approaches QUEENIE and tentatively puts a hand on her shoulder. QUEENIE flinches. SHIRLEY withdraws her hand.

SHIRLEY   You do know who I am, don't you? You were talking to me just now, weren't you? When you said it would be for the best?

QUEENIE can't speak.

            I know you were. You said exactly the same to me fifty years ago.

QUEENIE   Nnnnggg -

OLLIE   You what?

SHIRLEY   I didn't recognise you at first. How would I? I never saw you again, after the accident.

QUEENIE   Gggnnnn -

SHIRLEY   Your name wasn't Queenie then. It was -

QUEENIE   NNNHHHHH -

SHIRLEY   Well it doesn't really matter now, does it? None of that matters now. Except what it means to us.

OLLIE   What are you saying? D'you mean you two - did you use to be an item?

SHIRLEY   I wish. We were just the best of friends, from our first day at secretarial college. She turned up wearing a flying jacket and goggles. And she saw me looking curiously at her and she said: Oh, you mean this isn't the Secret Aerial College?

OLLIE's blank.

                Secret *Aerial* College?

She flaps her arms like wings. OLLIE's no wiser.

                Like aerial, as in flying?

OLLIE   Oh. *Aerial.* I thought you meant - *(Points a line above her head with a finger)* you know, as in sticky-up thing?

SHIRLEY   No.

OLLIE   Right.

SHIRLEY   I got it straight away and I laughed out loud - and that's how we just clicked. Of course it turned out she'd come on her motorbike, that's why she was / wearing -

OLLIE   Who - what - just a minute - Queenie? She had a *motor* bike?

SHIRLEY   She had this beautiful red motorbike. A Triumph Speed Twin. She told me her dad had bought it for her twenty-first. Which I also thought was quite fascinatingly curious. Anyway, that's what we used to call ourselves - The Speed Twins. I was the blonde one, she was the brunette. And we just basically used to glam ourselves up to the eyeballs and speed about on it - and, well, just basically drive boys wild for us. It was so exciting! We thought we were the absolute bee's knees - *(To QUEENIE)* didn't we? *(No response)* Well we just completely fell in love with *being us*. Until I nearly went and spoilt it all by trying to kiss her... She did kiss me back - she made it *her* kissing *me* - but then afterwards she said we mustn't ever do that again or we would corrupt ourselves. So I absolutely agreed with her, but of course I didn't really. Every time we even brushed bare arms after that I felt my whole insides go whoosh. So you can imagine what it was like, back on the bike, holding on to her waist, breathing into her neck, pressing my bosom up close to her back, this big throbbing thing between our thighs...

SHIRLEY sighs. QUEENIE groans. OLLIE turns away, loosening her collar.

OLLIE   Oh god I need a drink. And a smoke.

She takes out her soggy cigar and box of matches.

SHIRLEY	Then we had the accident. Because she thought this little dog was going to run out in front of us. So she swerved and we skidded - and three days later I woke up in hospital...
OLLIE	Right, yep, to find all your hopes and dreams in etcetera. Boop-a-do...
SHIRLEY	What are you doing?
OLLIE	Just seeing if I can dry out this soggy cigar. With a view to salvaging a modicum of happiness.

She strikes a match and rolls the cigar over the flame. SHIRLEY's aghast.

SHIRLEY	Oh please don't do that. She hates cigars.
OLLIE	I'm hoping the smell might restore her powers of speech.
SHIRLEY	She used to say they looked like the Devil's penis...
OLLIE	What?
SHIRLEY	Cigars. She used to say about cigars -
OLLIE	Yes I got the connection. I'm expressing revulsion. At the concept.
SHIRLEY	I think she may have been sexually abused as a child.
QUEENIE	Nnnnrrrggghhh -

OLLIE looks up again - and burns her fingers on the flame.

OLLIE   Ow, fuck! *(Blows out the match)* Oh this is doing my head.

SHIRLEY   It didn't occur to me then. But over the years - all these priests - well, don't you think that might explain…?

OLLIE slings the cigar aside.

OLLIE   Look, you know what, Shirley? Call me heartless, call me crass, call me any bad name you like, but I don't want to have to think about any of these depressing topics. I can feel myself teetering over an edge here. As in great gaping hideous stinking abyss. And I'm sorry, but I refuse to go anywhere near it, ever a-bloody-gain.

SHIRLEY   But you can't just ignore it, as if it doesn't exist.

OLLIE   I know it *exists*, Missy. I've more than done my life's bit for suffering humanity. And its multitude of suffering cousins. I've tried to save the whale, the battery chicken, the working donkey - the whole Noah's poor bloody Ark-load. Look at me! I'm worn out with caring about the infinite variety and oh so hideous specificity of suffering beings. All I want now is just to have a good time, you know? No opening up old wounds. Just to sit and chat about

> this 'n' that, to have a dance, a bit of harmless flirtation - and to *drink*. So please, before I lose my last thread of hope, will you kindly direct her bloody majesty to *(shouts at QUEENIE)* say she's sorry!

Pause. SHIRLEY's shocked into silence. QUEENIE clutches her head, making low moan. OLLIE despairs of them.

> Oh you two do what you like. I'm going to hunt for a key.

She goes behind the bar and out of sight.

The light closes in around SHIRLEY and QUEENIE. QUEENIE shakes and moans, head still in her hands.

SHIRLEY   Oh what am I to do with you? I can't just watch you suffer. You'll break my heart all over again.

QUEENIE sways. SHIRLEY grabs hold of her and leads her towards a seat.

> Sit down. There's nothing to be afraid of now.

QUEENIE   *(Hisses)* I'm not afraid. I just wanted that horrible old witch to leave us alone.

SHIRLEY   I can't believe you're finally saying you want to be alone with me.

QUEENIE   I couldn't bear you saying all those private things in front of her. You know I never wanted anyone to pry into that. And when I heard how you've let your own fancies delude you…? I knew you'd find me if you could. You never stopped trying. Even on my death bed. Sending your daughter to see me? That was unforgiveable.

SHIRLEY   What?

QUEENIE   Well somebody claiming to be your daughter came to see me. Looking the spit of you, according to Nursie. She brought me that old photo of us, on the bike.

SHIRLEY   My daughter Angelica brought you that old photo of us?

QUEENIE   Oh stop pretending you're surprised.

SHIRLEY   I am. I didn't send her. I was on my own death bed.

QUEENIE   Well I refused to see her. I had to pretend I was unconscious.

SHIRLEY   Why wouldn't you see her?

QUEENIE   Why would I see *her* if I'd made a lifelong vow not to see *you*?

SHIRLEY   My sweet baby girl. She must have been hoping you would send me a sign. Something to make it all meaningful at last…

She chokes up.

> Only you could hurt me like this.

QUEENIE   I didn't want to see my own daughter, never mind yours.

SHIRLEY looks at QUEENIE anew.

SHIRLEY   You wouldn't see your own daughter? On your death bed?

QUEENIE   Oh don't think I've not had my share of suffering. Don't ever think the choices I made were easy. That's how I know they were right, Shirley. And that's all that matters - to be able to stand before God on the Day of Judgement and say 'I did my best. I always did my best to do the right thing.'

Then she suddenly takes a deep and painful inhalation of breath, like a death rattle.

She gapes for a long, panicked moment, then makes a rasping exhalation, as if expelling a lungful of poisons.

SHIRLEY   Oh don't you see what you're doing to yourself? Still!

QUEENIE starts to hyperventilate again. SHIRLEY's angry now.

> I'll give you something to choke on. If my Angelica found that photo, she'll have found my diary...

QUEENIE looks up at her, aghast and gasping.

> And if she found you, she'll find your daughter. And they'll both know everything.

And QUEENIE flies at SHIRLEY with flailing arms.

QUEENIE   Nnnghhh - gggaaarrr - nnnhhhggg -

Then she rasps and gasps, as if she would die another death there and then.

SHIRLEY   Oh you fool!

She pulls QUEENIE into a mouth-to-mouth kiss. QUEENIE's too weak to resist. But it's as if she's receiving the kiss of life. Which turns into the passionate kiss of a lifetime...

Which is what OLLIE sees as she crawls from behind the bar, minus her bowler hat.

OLLIE   Well-halle-finally-bloody-lujah!

QUEENIE springs apart from SHIRLEY.

> Oh don't mind me, I'm in my own element. Found this under the bar.

She brandishes a bottle.

> Ouzo. Always the bottle of last resort but like a long-lost lover to me.

She kisses the bottle, opens it, and sits back against the bar to chug it back.

QUEENIE and SHIRLEY stand, looking out, neither knowing how to be next.

OLLIE chortles.

> You two put me in mind of a joke a Chinese doctor once told me. Well he told me two, actually. *(Glug)* I remember neither of them was remotely Chinese. *(Glug)* Ah yes! Here's one. Why is a football match better than sex? Why is a football match better than sex? Because you get forty-five minutes each way *and* a brass band at halftime. Boo-boom.

QUEENIE and SHIRLEY don't respond. OLLIE shrugs and glugs.

> That's not the one you put me in mind of, though. What's the other one? Oh damn... *(Glugs)* Ah yes! Two men in a bar. Two men in a bar. An Englishman and a Frenchman. And the Englishman says to the Frenchman, he says: *(Posh English accent)* Tell me, dear fellow, what exactly is the difference between our expression 'cool as a cucumber' and your expression 'song-fwar'? *(Glugs. Own voice)* So then the Frenchman says to the Englishman, he says: *(French accent)* I will tell you ze difference, mon ami. A man comes home from work to find his wife in bed wiz her lover. And if he does not fly into a rage

> but merely shrugs and says 'Je vous en prie, carry on' - zat is 'cool as a cucumber'. But zen if ze lover, he *can* carry on - *zat* is 'sang-froid'.

QUEENIE and SHIRLEY stay frozen.

> Well you see why you put me in mind of it.

Then comes a burst of glittering lights, like fireworks, and a blast of 'Ode To Joy' from the jukebox.

All three women are taken aback.

Then the bottle of Ouzo glows, as if filled with sparkling light.

> Eh?

The music resolves in a flourish and the lighting state reverts. OLLIE picks up the bottle and peers into it. Dips her finger in and sucks it.

> You'll never guess what? They've topped up my Ouzo and turned it into gin! Told you we were here to enjoy ourselves. Bugger you, Queenie.

She makes her way round the bar to mix a couple of drinks.

QUEENIE turns on her.

QUEENIE How dare you soil us with your perverted imagination! I was having an asthma attack, nothing to joke about. In the absence of an inhaler, Shirley was giving me mouth-to-mouth resuscitation.

OLLIE   Boop-a-do, boop-a-do.

SHIRLEY's dismayed.

SHIRLEY   *(To QUEENIE)* You traitor!

QUEENIE pushes her away, distraught.

QUEENIE   Leave me alone!

SHIRLEY   We're meant to be together, that's why we're here.

QUEENIE   Oh don't make me mad. Look at me! Dressed as a bloody beauty queen? I'm an old crone.

SHIRLEY   I know you're still you.

QUEENIE   Look! *(Rips off her wig, revealing her stubbly pate)* I haven't even got my own hair thanks to bloody chemo. Why the hell I bothered with all that... Oh you're so fortunate, Shirley, however you did it - to have your youthful looks... You're like a cruel mirror, to remind me of what I had and can never get back.

SHIRLEY   But you can. You know. You felt it.

QUEENIE   I don't want to feel *that*. I don't - I won't!

OLLIE   At least stick your wig back on while we still have to look at you.

QUEENIE throws her wig at SHIRLEY, who catches it and stares back at her, sorrowfully. OLLIE sighs as she fills another glass.

>Okey-dokes... Must be a fool to myself...

She serves up drinks.

>G & T for three. Chin-chin.

Neither SHIRLEY nor QUEENIE moves.

>Oh come and cheer yourselves up. While I'm feeling generous.

QUEENIE turns away, closing in on herself. SHIRLEY regards her with pity and disdain.

SHIRLEY   All she wants is to stay on her cross and suffer.

She throws the wig back at QUEENIE and joins OLLIE at the bar, choked up.

>She really is dead to me, isn't she?

OLLIE   Can't have an after-life if you've got no spirit.

SHIRLEY   Well I'm not waiting another eternity for her to change. I'm finished with her.

OLLIE   That's my girl! *(Hands her a glass and raises her own)* I propose a toast of thanks. To whom or whatever. For all good gifts.

SHIRLEY   *(Raising a glass, tearfully)* For all good gifts.

They clink and drink. Then OLLIE tips half of QUEENIE's glass into each of theirs.

OLLIE	Waste not, want not.
SHIRLEY	Did you ever love and lose, Ollie?
OLLIE	Me?
SHIRLEY	Someone special? Who broke your heart?
OLLIE	Bought the T-shirt and wore it out, dear.
SHIRLEY	What was her name? What happened?
OLLIE	Boop-a-do…
SHIRLEY	Oh don't pretend you can't remember -
OLLIE	Look - *(raising her glass)* we didn't get given this for being maudlin. Let's just be grateful for where we are.

But SHIRLEY insists, putting a hand on OLLIE's arm.

SHIRLEY	Please, Ollie - tell me.

OLLIE heaves a sigh.

OLLIE	This is so long ago. Might as well be somebody else's life…

Takes a swig.

> Her name was Joy. And she *was* a joy to me. She was an actress - starring on the gents' perfume counter in Harrod's when we met. Sprayed me with Eau Sauvage and we got chatting - and I told her I was

	in theatre, too - but of the operating variety…
SHIRLEY	You were a nurse?
OLLIE	I said I'm the type who prefers my patients unconscious, no 'angel' - and she gives me her number and says to call if ever I fancy doing a night shift…

Intake of excited breath from SHIRLEY.

	Well - typical dykes - one night of passion and she moves in - with her bags and her cats - and *stays* - for three happy years. Lifetime record for yours truly…
SHIRLEY	So why - what made you break up?

OLLIE sighs.

OLLIE	We went down the Gates one night - and there was this notice up: 'Anyone interested in being in the film *The Killing Of Sister George*, see Gina.'

SHIRLEY gasps, hands to face.

	Well anyone with any sense ran a mile. But it was Joy's dream come true. Being in a Hollywood movie? For thirty-seven quid a week? That was real money then.
SHIRLEY	Wonderful!
OLLIE	So she wanted us to take our summer holiday to be extras.

SHIRLEY   So you mean - you were *in it?*

OLLIE   *(Scoffs)* I said she was off her rocker. Me? Expose myself as a raving lesbian coming soon to a cinema near Matron? I said I wouldn't stop *her* but sorry, I was off to Greece to get a tan. I thought she'd think twice herself, if she thought about our landlord... But then they offered her a speaking part - for twenty-five quid a *day.*

Intake of breath from SHIRLEY.

So that was that. I went off on my hols, she stayed behind - just had to each do our own thing.

Beat.

SHIRLEY   You mean that was why you broke up? Because of the film?

OLLIE   No, because of me.

SHIRLEY exhales a puzzled breath - Why? What?

OLLIE takes a swig - and QUEENIE's turned her head to listen.

I was in my hotel room in Mykonos - in bed with this luscious young waitress, legs akimbo. Knock-knock at the door - in walks Joy.

SHIRLEY   Joy?

OLLIE   *(Jazz hands)* Surprise!

SHIRLEY gasps. QUEENIE's rigid. OLLIE shrugs and swigs.

SHIRLEY   She came out to Greece?

OLLIE   Chucked the film to be with me - to prove her love.

SHIRLEY gasps again, hands to face.

OLLIE   (*At QUEENIE*) And no, couldn't muster any *sang-froid* myself, in the circs.

She chokes up.

           Broke her heart. Then broke my own. Bloody fool…

SHIRLEY   Oh Ollie -

OLLIE   Oh fuck it.

She takes out her hanky and has a noisy blow.

And QUEENIE suddenly makes a stumbling exit through the loo door. SHIRLEY and OLLIE watch her go.

SHIRLEY   Should I go after her?

OLLIE pockets her hanky.

OLLIE   Let's just drown our sorrows in gin.

She tops up their glasses from the bottle, then raises hers.

           To Oblivion!

SHIRLEY raises her glass - and as they clink the jukebox lights up and starts playing The Marvellettes 'Forever'. SHIRLEY's struck.

SHIRLEY   It's playing my song.

OLLIE   'Your' song?

SHIRLEY   I always used to play this song after she left me…

OLLIE   Well what d'you know? Used to be one of our faves down the Gates. Pack the floor, a slow smooch.

SHIRLEY   I'd have loved to dance to this. Here. Then. If only I could be how I should have been.

OLLIE   Well, can still give it a twirl, eh?

She makes a formal bow, clicks her heels, and holds out her hand to SHIRLEY.

May I teach you 'The Gateways Grind'?

A beat - as SHIRLEY sends a last look to the loo door, after QUEENIE - then she plays her part with OLLIE.

SHIRLEY   I thought you'd never ask.

OLLIE steers her over to the dance floor, as the bar disappears into shadow.

OLLIE pulls SHIRLEY into a close smooch, SHIRLEY's hands on OLLIE's shoulders, OLLIE's round her waist and a leg between SHIRLEY's thighs, and they abandon themselves to the intimate dance.

The music increases in volume and the lights dim lower.

In the middle section of the song OLLIE twirls SHIRLEY away and hand-mimes to the lyrics in camp Dusty Springfield fashion, playing the love slave for SHIRLEY's amusement.

As the song fades out, SHIRLEY and OLLIE stand still for a moment, both a bit overwhelmed.

SHIRLEY   That was - fab!

OLLIE   Smashing!

Beat.

            You know, Shirley, you really are a peach. If only I'd met you back then.

SHIRLEY   I wasn't half as bold when I was really young. This is me with the benefit of fifty years of regrets.

OLLIE   Ah yes, I forget.

SHIRLEY   Do let's.

She gives OLLIE a kiss on the cheek.

            Thank you.

OLLIE   Thank *you*.

QUEENIE   Thank *me*. It's my girl you danced with.

The lights come back up - and we see QUEENIE lounging in the loo doorway, backlit like a film star. She's transformed - wearing a Coral Browne short-haired wig and a tailored trouser-suit, white shirt and black tie.

OLLIE and SHIRLEY gape.

SHIRLEY   Oh my!

OLLIE   Queenie?

QUEENIE   The name's Bobby.

SHIRLEY   That's what she always used to call herself.

QUEENIE raises a lighted cigarette to her lips. SHIRLEY thrills.

              Oh you're not - !

OLLIE   You *what*?

QUEENIE exhales a plume of smoke with flair.

SHIRLEY   Oh my!

QUEENIE regards the cigarette.

QUEENIE.   Muratti Ariston. My favourite.

SHIRLEY   I *knew* that would be your brand.

QUEENIE   I always knew you'd be my girl.

QUEENIE winks. OLLIE bristles.

OLLIE   Just a bloody minute, ducky -

QUEENIE arches an eyebrow. OLLIE takes a gulp of her drink and muscles over.

              What the hell do you think you're playing at? You can't just swan back here in a suit and *smoke*!

QUEENIE   It's just the one. For effect.

QUEENIE puts the cigarette in her mouth and waves her hands.

>Look, no hands.

SHIRLEY titters.

>If I'm going to damn myself at least I can do it with style.

OLLIE Well don't think you're getting back in with her. She's finished with you for keeps. I'm the lucky feller now.

QUEENIE Oh catch up. You're no match for me in Armani.

OLLIE Tell her, Shirley. Tell her she can take a running jump.

No response. OLLIE turns to see SHIRLEY looking sheepish.

>Eh? Come on. She had her last chance with you. Went and left you in the lurch.

SHIRLEY I know. But now she's come back the way I always wanted her to be.

OLLIE *(To QUEENIE)* Well over my dead body.

QUEENIE exhales in OLLIE's face.

QUEENIE Why don't you slip silently away and have a sulk in the lavs?

She pushes past, dropping her cigarette in OLLIE's drink, and holds her hand out to SHIRLEY.

>   Come on, Shirley. Let's make up for lost time.

She takes wide-eyed SHIRLEY by the hand and twirls her over to the banquette. OLLIE flares.

OLLIE   Right, so you want a fight, eh? Eh?

She puts up her fists.

>   Well come on then, stick 'em up. I'll give you a good fight.

QUEENIE   Oh don't be pathetic. Just *go*.

OLLIE   Oh nunna - nunna - na. You don't understand the rules, matey. I get off with your bird, you want her back - you have to fight me for her.

SHIRLEY   But I don't want you to *fight*.

OLLIE   Not your business, girly. This is between me and 'Bobby'.

QUEENIE   There's *nothing* between you and me, you drunken old frump. I'm not even listening to you.

OLLIE   Well listen to this.

She grabs her drink and slings it over QUEENIE. SHIRLEY gasps.

SHIRLEY   Oh no -

QUEENIE stiffens, OLLIE bays and sways.

OLLIE   Aw, has her Armani gone all soggy? Oh boo-hoo-hoo. Tell the big drip to go hang, Shirley, and come back to me.

And QUEENIE's on her feet, glowering with pent-up menace.

QUEENIE   Oh don't be ridiculous! Look at yourself, you grotesque swaggering ape. If you had any sense of shame you'd *want* to hide yourself away.

OLLIE sways, SHIRLEY flinches.

OLLIE   Right, get your jacket off - you've had it, you -

SHIRLEY   *(To QUEENIE)* Say you didn't mean that -

OLLIE   *(Struggling to strip off her jacket)* You put your mitts where your mouth is, you stuck-up ponce. Come on! I'll wipe the sneer off your prissy face, you - (*Gets her arms tangled in her braces*) - shitting bollocks pissing fuck shit -

She stumbles against the bar, arms trussed - and slumps, defeated.

QUEENIE   I rest my case.

SHIRLEY   Don't be horrid to her - say you're sorry.

QUEENIE   Me? I'm not the one with a King Kong complex.

She flourishes a handkerchief and sits back on the banquette to dab herself down. SHIRLEY flusters, looking from one to the other… tries to make light.

SHIRLEY   Honestly - what am I to do with you pair of silly billies? One of you, quickly, come on - just say you're sorry and make everything nice again… Oh come on, you can't leave me like this… *(To QUEENIE)* Oh please don't spoil it all…

OLLIE's up-standing.

OLLIE   Down to me, girly - I'll do the honours… *(Straightens herself up, makes a dignified bow)* Apologies to both of you. My fault, what just happened. Same old Muggins… All comes back to me now - how I got myself banned the last time round… Bad form, smacky botty, won't give you any more trouble.

SHIRLEY watches as OLLIE clambers on to a bar stool, collects SHIRLEY's abandoned glass, tops it up from the Ouzo bottle and takes a slug - and dims into shadow with her back turned on them.

SHIRLEY   Poor Ollie… But that was awfully big of her, wasn't it?

The banquette is romantically lit but QUEENIE's silent. SHIRLEY flounces.

> Oh don't you dare go all moody on me now... You've got some big-time making-up to do, you.

She sits beside QUEENIE, all feisty/flirty.

> Making me wait all this time for you to finally make your move? Well you're lucky if I let you try, so don't take it for granted. You'd better sweep me off my feet...

QUEENIE's rigid. SHIRLEY gives her a nudge.

SHIRLEY   Did you hear me?

OLLIE takes a look over her shoulder.

OLLIE   Hah! I knew it. She's all piss and no poke. *(Pulls herself up)* Sorry, sorry.

Turns her back again. QUEENIE gets to her feet, grim-faced, heads towards the loo door. SHIRLEY's outraged.

SHIRLEY   You're not going to flunk it *again*?

QUEENIE   I need to talk to you - in private.

SHIRLEY   I don't want to *talk* - in the toilet? I want to be here - now - out on a date with you. Oh come on, you've got the look, act the part.

QUEENIE   You don't even know the half of me, do you? You really think we could start again, Shirley - forgive and forget - just like that?

SHIRLEY   No. Obviously I will have to punish you... Preferably in a leather-look dominatrix costume with stiletto boots and a whip... I'm going to tie you down and turn you on till you're *begging* to be allowed to fuck me.

QUEENIE recoils. OLLIE nearly falls off her bar stool.

OLLIE   Bloody hell! You really are a live one, girly.

SHIRLEY stamps her foot at QUEENIE.

SHIRLEY   Go crazy for me! What's the matter with you?

QUEENIE   Oh stop being so bloody *young*!

She pushes away. SHIRLEY stares after her, shaking her head in dismay, then clutches her lame leg, as if feeling a sudden spasm of pain.

OLLIE   Aw pet -

SHIRLEY   Oh I'm mad to try and keep our flame alight. Look at her! She'll never have the nerve to be wild again.

OLLIE   Leave her to rot in her own box, then. I'm sure I'm no stranger to a spot of spanky-panky. Fantasy fetish wear - my speciality! Butch on the streets, easy-osy between the sheets - yours to command, eh? Few more of these...

She gulps her drink and tops it up from the Ouzo bottle. SHIRLEY pursues QUEENIE.

SHIRLEY   You know this is your very last chance with me? It's really it. If you don't reach out to me now...

QUEENIE detaches herself, as if having a different conversation - in a determinedly bright tone.

QUEENIE   I think my husband was the closest I had to a true friend. We always backed each other up. That was our pact. Even when he knew I didn't desire him, he commiserated with my medical excuses. He was even willing to blame himself for our only daughter becoming a lesbian...

SHIRLEY   What?

OLLIE splutters over her drink.

OLLIE   Excuse me, but did she just say - ?

QUEENIE   *(Snaps)* I revealed a painful truth. Spare me your mockery.

SHIRLEY   I'm not mocking, I - I'm -

OLLIE   You gave birth to a little lezzer? I'm bloody pissing myself.

QUEENIE   *(To SHIRLEY)* Well there, now you know how hard I've been tested.

SHIRLEY turns on her, urgent.

SHIRLEY   What did you say to her, when she told you? Tell me what you said to her!

QUEENIE   I said she was taking the easy way out.

OLLIE   *(Starting to slur)* Well you gave yourself away there, Queenie. Who but a lesbian would appreciate the temptation?

QUEENIE ignores OLLIE, makes her way over to a seat. SHIRLEY pursues.

SHIRLEY   What else?

QUEENIE   I told her I didn't want to see her ever again unless she promised to give it up.

SHIRLEY   Oh no…

QUEENIE   She kept on pestering me with phone calls. Letters. Sending me photos of her and her 'partner'. Begging me to let them visit so I could see for myself how *nice* she was, how happy they were together. Then she told me they were getting 'married'. Would I come? Well I'm sure you can understand now, Shirley, why I had to cut her off completely and hold out to the bitter end.

SHIRLEY   You mean - she didn't even know you were ill?

QUEENIE   I instructed the nurse that I no longer acknowledged my daughter as next-of-kin.

SHIRLEY   And you dare - you dare call Ollie 'grotesque'?

OLLIE belches loudly.

OLLIE   Pardon.

SHIRLEY   *(To QUEENIE)* Well you're a monster! You really are.

QUEENIE turns on them, angry.

QUEENIE   What was I supposed to do when my only daughter wants a wedding with two brides? Proudly announce it to all my friends at the bridge club? Weeping tears of joy? I had a duty to be tough - to test *her*, to do all I could to try and help her grow out of it.

She falters.

OLLIE   *(Snorts)* 'Grow out of it'! *(To SHIRLEY)* Does she think it's a dress size?

SHIRLEY   She thinks her 'principles' are more important than people.

QUEENIE   You want to know what I honestly think, Shirley - now?

She gathers herself.

I think the real pity is I didn't die in that accident. If only, hmm? Then you could have mourned me and got over it, to go in pursuit of some other woman, if that was your compulsion. My poor husband would have found an uncomplicated wife, like all the other young men I refused - because I was pursued by quite a few, as you can imagine, once I turned my back on you. And my daughter - well, she would have been lucky never to have been mine. There! All I really have to regret is my death came so late in my life.

OLLIE raises her glass, swaying on her stool.

OLLIE   Cheerio!

SHIRLEY   Yes, if only that were true.

QUEENIE   It's true enough for me now.

SHIRLEY   It's not true! All we can regret are our *choices*.

QUEENIE   Oh will you ever stop goading me!

SHIRLEY   You need me to.

QUEENIE   Your mission's accomplished, Shirley. I've confessed my remaining sins. Now I can drink myself as stupid as Ollie -

OLLIE   Huh?

QUEENIE   - but know that my soul is cleansed, come what still may, even yet.

SHIRLEY   What?!

OLLIE   *(To QUEENIE)* Don't think you're drinking any more of *my* drink.

SHIRLEY   You still think you're going to Heaven?

QUEENIE   God moves in mysterious ways.

SHIRLEY beats her fists on the bar, howling with frustration.

SHIRLEY   Stop lying to yourself!

QUEENIE recoils.

QUEENIE   Have you lost your mind?

SHIRLEY   You are such a pathetic coward.

OLLIE jeers at QUEENIE.

OLLIE   Yowzer!

QUEENIE   Coward? Me? I think I'm the bravest bloody person I've ever met.

SHIRLEY   Ollie's worth ten of you. She's the one who lived the brave life, not you.

OLLIE   Doof!

SHIRLEY   It was you who *chose* the easy way out - to hide behind the church and pretend to be 'normal'. Except I knew it wasn't as easy as you'd hoped, living a lie, didn't I? Because I was living it too. And I wrote to you - how many times? Before either of us had children I tried so hard to make you give us another chance. And all you ever

> sent me back was a two-line note - to tell me you were sorry if I was unhappy but I was completely wrong to think we'd ever been more than friends - and if I couldn't control my unhealthy feelings then I should go and see a doctor.

She's shaking with anger.

> You cut off your daughter because you were *jealous* of her happiness. You were scared she would prove how you'd wasted your own life and the love *we* had. And you wish it was *me* who'd died in that accident. So you could have buried your guilt with me.

QUEENIE rounds on OLLIE.

QUEENIE   Give me that bloody bottle!

OLLIE gives her the finger and a raspberry.

SHIRLEY   I need you to be *you*, so I can be *me*.

OLLIE   *(To SHIRLEY, confused)* You don't need her to be you. Eh? Bollocks. *(To QUEENIE)* Just tell her she's free to go with me. *(Stumbles)* Whoops!

QUEENIE dives for the bottle -

QUEENIE   Give me that -

- but OLLIE clings on to it.

OLLIE   Gerroff!

QUEENIE   Give me the gin!

OLLIE   Gimme the girl!

As they wrestle violently over the bottle the lighting state turns red. SHIRLEY clutches her head in despair.

SHIRLEY   Oh STOP THIS!

She looks around in horror.

            Look what we're doing…

OLLIE's given sobering pause for thought. QUEENIE resists.

QUEENIE   We're all just overwrought.

A commanding organ chord from the jukebox overrules, and a bright light shines on a hitherto unnoticed plinth upon which sits a parchment scroll.

OLLIE   What's that then?

They all stare at it.

SHIRLEY   *(To QUEENIE)* Will you go and look?

QUEENIE   *(At OLLIE)* She can go and look, if she's the 'brave' one.

OLLIE rises to the challenge, makes her way to the plinth with her bottle, puts that on the plinth as she picks up the parchment, un-scrolls it and reads. Low organ music continues under. SHIRLEY and QUEENIE await her reaction. OLLIE carries on reading, giving nothing away.

SHIRLEY   What does it say, Ollie?

No response. SHIRLEY looks to QUEENIE.

> Don't you want to know?

QUEENIE I'm sure I can guess. She was right, I was wrong. *(To OLLIE)* Just bring back the bottle. Let's all get boozed and blank out.

OLLIE looks up from the scroll, in a state of shock.

OLLIE We can't now. We've got to go *back*.

SHIRLEY *(To QUEENIE)* See, *I* was right! We've got to go back over the past before we can go forward.

OLLIE No, we've got to go back to the bloody future...

SHIRLEY Sorry?

OLLIE holds up the scroll and reads aloud in a graveyard voice.

OLLIE 'To whom it may concern. Your time here is coming to an end. We hope you will use this opportunity for self-healing and reflection in order to prepare for your rebirth.'

SHIRLEY Sorry?

QUEENIE *Rebirth?*

OLLIE 'We know this will be a difficult adjustment for you all, particularly those of you who still cling to false beliefs. But

	you have a degree of choice as to your next incarnation.'
SHIRLEY	Sorry?
QUEENIE	*Choice?*
OLLIE	'As the time approaches for you to reincarnate, you will begin to feel an increasing attachment to your natural tendencies and to familiar sensations. If, for example, you lived a life as a seaman, you may again be drawn to incarnate near an ocean.'
SHIRLEY	…?
QUEENIE	*What?*
OLLIE	'Or you may reject the choices of your past life and seek to apply new lessons learned whilst here in the spirit world. In the final analysis, it is - quotes - 'who you really are' - unquotes - that decides the path ahead.'
	Then there's a star and it says 'some text missing'.
QUEENIE	It's got to be a joke.

There's a thunderous organ chord.

OLLIE	I don't think it's a joke.
SHIRLEY	What you mean - you mean we have to go back - to earth - and - live all over again?

OLLIE   Anew.

QUEENIE   That's impossible. It's *heathen*.

Another even louder chord - and the scroll jolts in OLLIE's hands. She stares at it.

OLLIE   The last bit's come through… It says 'Step One - accept that the comfort of alcohol is an illusion.'

A resounding CRACK and the bottle on the plinth explodes, spectacularly.

The three women quake as the organ music swells then cuts out.

Blackout.

End of Act 1.

ACT TWO

The jukebox plays 'Cast Your Fate to the Wind' by Sounds Orchestral.

The set is as before, the lighting state spectral.

The three women sit separately, and desolately, each with a clipboard and pen.

OLLIE and QUEENIE have both removed their jackets, loosened their ties and rolled up their shirt-sleeves.

The atmosphere is very tense, as the music fades down and out.

Then QUEENIE bangs down her pen.

QUEENIE   Oh this is preposterous!

OLLIE   I'm trying to concentrate.

SHIRLEY   We can't argue with it. It's compulsory.

QUEENIE   Having to fill in a multiple choice questionnaire about who you want to be in the next life? It's *unthinkable*.

OLLIE   Got to get bloody 'reborn' to get another bloody drink's all I can think.

SHIRLEY   We just have to approach it in the spirit of 'which would you rather'. *(QUEENIE scoffs)* Even if it all sounds ghastly there's always a preference, if you have to choose. I definitely know, for instance, I'd rather be reborn into a nice white middle class

	family in Dorset than take my chances anywhere foreign. And I don't think that's racist. It's just being sensible.
QUEENIE	How do you know what's sensible? Most of the world could be speaking Standard Mandarin by the time we've grown up again. The whole of the Home Counties could be a desert if the suicide bombers go nuclear. Then there's global warming, pollution, all the wrong people having more and more offspring... Bloody robots could end up in charge of everything, for all we know.
OLLIE	We don't seem to have that option, to return as a robot.
QUEENIE	How can we choose to return as anything? How can we possibly know what's for the best?
OLLIE	'Least you sound as if you're rejecting the Catholic policy on birth control.
QUEENIE	Well of course I reject - Oh you non-Catholics don't understand. After Vatican Two - oh just shut up about religion, will you?
OLLIE	It's a box we've got to tick. Are you ticking 'None'?
QUEENIE	I don't have to tell you what I'm ticking.

SHIRLEY   It's really hard, that one, isn't it? I'm wondering if I should tick 'Hindu' now? Or 'Buddhist'?

QUEENIE   What?

SHIRLEY   Well they were the only ones who basically got it right? About reincarnation?

QUEENIE   Why have you suddenly adopted that irritating upward inflection?

SHIRLEY   Have I? I don't know. Because everything suddenly feels so - uncertain?

OLLIE   I'm not surprised - chances of finding a nice white middle class Hindu family in Dorset.

SHIRLEY   Oh I don't know what to choose now. I just wish we'd been told all this before. That this was how it was all going to work out. It's such a total shock, when I was only just reclaiming who I was…

OLLIE   So you can tick that box, anyway. 'Sexuality'? Homo.

QUEENIE   Oh don't be ridiculous! If you *have* got a proper choice about it you wouldn't *choose* to be abnormal.

OLLIE   Well I'm not choosing to be anything else. Why would I choose to be hetero? Well, not unless I choose to be male…

SHIRLEY   You're going to choose to be male?

OLLIE   I'm astonished I didn't choose it last time round. At the age of five, I'm sure I would have. It was obvious to me by then that boys had the best deal.

SHIRLEY   What - you think - you think we *chose* to be who we were last time?

OLLIE   What we're supposed to think now, isn't it?

QUEENIE   Well that is beyond preposterous. As if I would have chosen to be *me*...

Pause for thought - as the fragments of mirror glint.

SHIRLEY   This is making me feel dizzy.

QUEENIE   Oh it's just absurd.

OLLIE makes a flourish with her pen. And again. SHIRLEY and QUEENIE attend.

SHIRLEY   What have you ticked, Ollie?

OLLIE   All options considered, Shirley, I can only conclude my inner me's got a built-in turn-off to male tackle. Even rubber jobs, before you ask. Nup. Just not my thing, never was, no can change, so there we go - yours truly is quintessentially dyke.

QUEENIE   Well lucky mum who gives birth to that bundle of joy.

SHIRLEY   Well I think I probably am too.

QUEENIE   You think you're what?

SHIRLEY   The same as Ollie. Basically.

QUEENIE   Don't be ridiculous, you're not remotely -

SHIRLEY   Well I must be, mustn't I? I've tried not to be but I couldn't stop myself having those feelings.

QUEENIE   But you're not a hopeless hard case like her. You'd only have to shift one degree, you could be perfectly normal.

SHIRLEY   Then maybe that's the crucial degree that makes me *me*. That gives me my vital spark.

QUEENIE   Oh rot! It's what's always stopped you being everything *else* you could be, isn't it? So why would you cling to it if you can tick a box and be rid of it?

SHIRLEY   I can't help it. It's just how I feel.

QUEENIE   But why? What do you mean?

OLLIE   Why should she have to *explain*?

SHIRLEY   Well I don't mind *trying* to explain - if she's interested in my answer?

QUEENIE   I'm utterly mystified, aren't I? Why would you want to pin your whole identity on

	the one abnormal bit of you that ruins all the rest?
SHIRLEY	Because it's what makes me fall in love. Well that's what it all comes down to. And I could never understand why people said 'opposites attract'. That wasn't my idea of romantic bliss. I wanted to be with someone I could share everything with, not feel separate and different from. So I always knew deep down it had to be another girl - just the type of girl to really make me swoon needed to be a bit more - well, you know - mannish.
QUEENIE	Well then all you need to find next time is a man who's a bit *less* mannish.
SHIRLEY	My husband was the gentlest man ever. He didn't even like football. And I loved him for loving me - and being a good father to our daughter. But he never made me swoon.
QUEENIE	Okay. Then he must have had a degree too much *un*-mannishness. But that's all it can be, to get the right match - just a question of degree. As it must be for me…
OLLIE	Sod you, Queenie. If you're not going to tell us what you're ticking, you can keep out of our discussion.
QUEENIE	But I think we *should* all discuss this.

OLLIE	Oh do you? Well tough titties.
SHIRLEY	No, I think we should, if she wants to. I'd love to know what she thinks she really is.
OLLIE	Not unless she tells us which box she's ticked for 'religion'. Because if she's ticked 'Catholic' again -
QUEENIE	I haven't ticked anything yet, actually.
SHIRLEY	Well what do you *think* you're going to tick for 'sexuality'? Are you just going to go for a hundred per cent hetero?

No response.

> Well are you or not?

OLLIE	Please, do tell.

QUEENIE avoids this question by answering a previous one.

QUEENIE	I wasn't sexually abused as a child, as a matter of fact, let alone by a priest. And there was a time when I *loved* the smell of cigar smoke, when I was a small child, because it was my darling Daddy's smell. I loved everything about his cigars - his beautiful old mahogany humidor, his Cuban cigar boxes with their coloured pictures, the shiny metal tubes they came in - and he used to let me trim his cigars for him with his silver cigar cutter... I loved all the paraphernalia of it. Until one day he said a terrible thing to me. He said

if only he could share his cigar with me, because he knew I'd love the taste as well as the smell. And I thought he just thought I was too scared to have a puff of it. And I said 'I'm not scared to smoke it, Daddy. May I please have a puff?' And he laughed at me. He just laughed at me. And he said 'If only you were a boy…' Well that was my moment like yours, Ollie. When I knew that it would be oh so infinitely better to have been a boy. That being a girl was so much *less*. And that there was nothing I could do about it. Except hate cigars forevermore.

Pause.

SHIRLEY   Really? You mean that's all it was?

QUEENIE   What do you mean 'that's all'? It was my first intimation of life's total unfairness.

SHIRLEY   Well I mean I'm glad you weren't sexually abused.

QUEENIE   I'm not saying I was *happy*.

OLLIE   So Queenie wanted to be a boy. Well there's an admission at last.

QUEENIE   Only because my Daddy would have preferred a son. But if girls and boys hadn't been treated so differently…

SHIRLEY   I never wanted to be a boy. I suppose I had brothers, unlike you. And my dad preferred me to all of them.

QUEENIE   Well I'm sure we all must have had moments of envy? Because of the unfairness.

OLLIE   I seem to recall that some of us did something about it. This unequal treatment of the sexes. What was it we did now? Oh yes. We became *feminists*.

QUEENIE   I didn't just put up with it. I got on. I travelled. I always believed in equal pay for equal work.

OLLIE   *(To SHIRLEY)* Remind me, which branch of feminism was it that used to go in for beauty competitions?

SHIRLEY   Don't be mean. She had a motorbike.

OLLIE   She had a motorbike.

QUEENIE   I *insisted* on having a motorbike.

OLLIE   Upon which you rode dolled up like a beauty queen for the allurement of boys? Huh!

QUEENIE   At least I proved I *could* allure them. I could have had the pick of them. I didn't have to seek out desperate places like this.

OLLIE	Oh now I'm just a dyke out of desperation?
SHIRLEY	Oh please don't let's argue.
OLLIE	I wondered how long it would take her to come up with that slur.
SHIRLEY	She doesn't mean it.
QUEENIE	I *do* mean it. Who could possibly aspire to this as a lifestyle? Furtive gatherings in dingy basements? Being an object of scorn and mockery? You'd have to be desperate.
OLLIE	You should've been revving it up with the dykes-on-bikes, darling.
SHIRLEY	Anyway it's not as bad nowadays, is it? If you can practically get married?
QUEENIE	What, you think two 'gays' going up the aisle will ever be on the same social par as a man and a woman? It's just *embarrassing*.
SHIRLEY	That's just you being old-fashioned.
QUEENIE	It's how it *is*.

OLLIE bangs down her clipboard.

OLLIE	Before you lecture us on what to do with our next set of genitalia, just tell us which you're going to tick. Male? Female? Or Intersex?

Beat.

SHIRLEY   She wouldn't tick that. Would you?

QUEENIE   Of course I'm not ticking that.

OLLIE   So which?

QUEENIE's back on the spot.

QUEENIE   *(To SHIRLEY)* What are you saying you're going to tick?

SHIRLEY takes a deep breath, then ticks her clipboard.

SHIRLEY   I'm ticking the same as Ollie. Sex: 'Female'. Sexuality: 'Homo'. Because that's who I am and who I want to be.

OLLIE   Bravo!

And a brief trumpet fanfare from the jukebox gives echo.

All the women startle.

                Forgot we weren't alone. *(Upwards)* Any chance of another illusory snifter? By way of celebration?

Another da-da-da-da blast and a light shines on the bar top - where there are two flutes of champagne waiting and a lighted cigarette in an ashtray.

SHIRLEY   Look! Champagne! And a cigarette!

OLLIE claps her hands together in joy.

OLLIE   See, it's never too late to come out.

SHIRLEY   *(Upwards)* Thank you!

OLLIE		*(Upwards)* Or 'Namaste' or whatever.

She scoots to the bar to grab a glass, followed by SHIRLEY.

(To SHIRLEY) Cheers to you, girlie!

SHIRLEY	I couldn't have decided without you, Ollie. Cheers!
OLLIE	Too bad for you, Queenie.

She takes a deep draw on the cigarette, then exhales in QUEENIE's direction.

QUEENIE	*(Turning away)* Oh please don't mind me.
OLLIE	Don't worry, we won't.

SHIRLEY pangs after QUEENIE.

SHIRLEY	We can't drink without her.
OLLIE	I can. Merrily. And smoke. Bliss.
SHIRLEY	*(To QUEENIE)* Oh come and have a sip of mine.
OLLIE	Let her earn her own bloody drink. *(To QUEENIE)* Go on, tick a box.
SHIRLEY	You have to be *something*.
QUEENIE	Do I? I wonder what would happen if I categorically refuse to choose.

A rumble of thunder.

(Upwards) This isn't a proper choice. Because it's not *informed*.

SHIRLEY   They said it's got to be about 'who you really are'. You must know what you *think* you really are? Just to tick the first two boxes?

OLLIE   And get your own glass of champers?

SHIRLEY   To be given a second chance?

QUEENIE clouds over, in her own existential whirl. Then snaps out of it.

QUEENIE   Oh what the hell! I am so utterly sick and tired of striving. So fine. All right. *(Ticking her clipboard)* 'Female'. 'Homo'. Happy?

Fireworks. Burst of 'Ode to Joy'. And another glass of champagne appears on top of the bar.

SHIRLEY   Look!

QUEENIE goes to grab the drink - and downs it in one.

               You don't think you should've made that last?

QUEENIE   What for? So they can use it for target practice?

OLLIE   Well don't think you're getting a sip of ours, when you get stuck on the next questions.

QUEENIE   Oh I'm just going with the flow now. Totally. Whatever you two tick, I'm ticking the same. What does it matter?

	It's ludicrous. Whatever will be will be, san fairy ann, who cares.
OLLIE	Well don't think that's not a choice. That you've just made. You've just chosen to take pot luck.
SHIRLEY	No. She's chosen to be with us. *(To QUEENIE)* Isn't that what you're really saying?
QUEENIE	Absolutely. I want us all to grow up as healthy little lesbians in a nice white middle-class Hindu ashram in Dorset and live happily ever after. Or get burned at the stake, whichever comes first.
SHIRLEY	Oh you! This is still so typically *you*, to sound all mocking and tough but be basically timid and conformist.
	(To OLLIE) This is so typically her, I can't tell you.
OLLIE	Tssk.
QUEENIE	I thought you said you wanted me to be *me*.
SHIRLEY	Not you as you *were*, you as you *could* be. You just won't ever, *ever* come to the fore.
QUEENIE	What do you mean, 'come to the fore'? 'Come to the fore'? You were the pillion passenger.

SHIRLEY   What, and you were 'the driver'? You were never really the driver. I kept on hoping you *would* be. Some fine day. I knew you wanted to be. You the brainy brunette. You the show off. You the quick wit and the sharp tongue. You wanted to be better than all the boys. But you just never had the courage. It was me who had the *courage*, to want us to be together. Wasn't it? Silly girly me. The blonde bimbo. And I knew I did have it, really, except I wanted *you* to have it. Even now, meeting you here, I really hoped, at last - *(She pulls back, tearful again)* Oh I'm so stupid. I can't believe I let you -

OLLIE   Hey, come on, pet. You were doing fine without her.

SHIRLEY   No, this is *me*. I'm a cripple.

She sits on a beer barrel, hugging her lame leg. OLLIE pursues.

OLLIE   No no, you won't have that thing on your leg next time.

SHIRLEY   I will. I will. I can't help it. I'm broken.

OLLIE   Hey, hey. Shush, shush. You'll be mended. There'll be a way.

SHIRLEY   Oh you're so sweet, Ollie / but -

OLLIE   You'll see. Got healing hands, me. Sure there's many a little broken bird I've saved in my time.

QUEENIE snaps.

QUEENIE   I thought you were hoping for another date with Princess Margaret.

OLLIE   *(Over SHIRLEY's shoulder)* Fuck Princess Margaret! *(Jolts)* Oh - is that déjà vu? *(At QUEENIE)* Well, as dying words go, beats 'Look out for Tufty!'

SHIRLEY   'Look out for Tufty'? Those were your…

OLLIE   Yep. Not 'Look out for Shirley'.

QUEENIE   It was the morphine…

SHIRLEY sobs into OLLIE's arms and QUEENIE turns away, swaying.

Oh my dear god - what have I done…?

And darkness descends - as QUEENIE finally catches up with herself, looking out into the void.

I left you with nothing. And my poor daughter…

And she breaks down - beating her chest and making hideous moan.

SHIRLEY is aghast, OLLIE repelled by the spectacle.

SHIRLEY   Oh no, oh no, oh no, oh please don't…

QUEENIE ignores, beating herself up.

SHIRLEY's distraught.

> Ollie, please stop her. Please stop her. Please stop her...

OLLIE snaps into no-nonsense nurse mode. Strides over to QUEENIE and shakes her.

OLLIE Stop this bloody exhibition right now!

QUEENIE carries on regardless.

> I said *stop it!*

She slaps QUEENIE round the face. QUEENIE gasps as she jolts out of her moment.

> For god's sake! We've all got a burden to carry. Stop bleating about it and be a bloody man.

QUEENIE's confused.

QUEENIE I'm not a man - I'm a mother.

OLLIE Well too late to fix that - so act like a bloody man. Show some fibre. *(Indicating SHIRLEY)* For *her.*

QUEENIE sways.

> Oh give yourself a shake. Or you'll be nothing to anybody.

QUEENIE collects herself.

QUEENIE I apologise. That was an inexcusable lapse.

OLLIE	We'll pretend it didn't happen. *(To SHIRLEY)* Didn't happen, okay?

SHIRLEY's uncertain.

	(To QUEENIE) Now you rise manfully to the challenge and get that bloody calliper off her leg.
QUEENIE	What?
OLLIE	You put it there, you get it off. Just bloody do it before I thump you.

QUEENIE galvanises, strides over to SHIRLEY and kneels in front of her.

QUEENIE	Rest your foot on my lap. I'll make you better.

SHIRLEY looks at OLLIE, bemused.

SHIRLEY	She thinks she can just - pull it off?
QUEENIE	Watch me.

QUEENIE wrestles with the calliper - then snaps it free. And there's a ripple of tinkling bells.

	There! Now stand up.
SHIRLEY	I can't walk without it.
QUEENIE	Give it a try, Shirley. Please? For me?

She holds out her hand for support. SHIRLEY wobbles to her feet, nearly falls.

SHIRLEY	Ooh!

QUEENIE holds her.

          I can't -

QUEENIE   You can -

SHIRLEY   I don't -

She sits back down, rubbing her lame leg, and QUEENIE reaches out to her.

QUEENIE   Let's go back and be us again, Shirley. Let's be The Speed Twins at our best. Then nothing could put out our spark, could it? We even went to the edge of nowhere - to go mad in the head off Malin Head - and be the only two human beings on a deserted little island...

SHIRLEY   You remember that?

QUEENIE   Everybody said we'd never make it, didn't they? Well that was us aimed and fired. Strapped our little suitcases on the back rack, opened the throttle and off we went to Holyhead - on the ferry to Ireland - then all the way up to the northernmost tip of Donegal... till we could see the lighthouse on Inishtrahull, no more than a few miles away over the Sound, but completely out of our reach - unless we could persuade those crusty old fishermen it wasn't bad luck to take women on their boat.

SHIRLEY   Well I hope it wasn't…

QUEENIE   Bad luck? We got there and back, didn't we?

SHIRLEY   But we don't know what happened to them afterwards…

She puts a teasing hand to her mouth - and QUEENIE copies.

QUEENIE   Oops!

Guilty girlish giggles.

SHIRLEY   That would be awful, wouldn't it? If they drowned…

QUEENIE   We'll have to hope they've reincarnated somewhere salty and fishy.

SHIRLEY.   But not near Dorset.

QUEENIE   Oops!

More giggles.

            We didn't mean them any harm. We can't feel guilty.

SHIRLEY   We ate all their sandwiches.

QUEENIE   We were hungry.

SHIRLEY   And we drank all their whiskey.

QUEENIE   And we gave them a thrill.

SHIRLEY   We were really naughty, weren't we?

QUEENIE   We were dazzling.

She takes SHIRLEY's hands.

>Oh come on, Shirley, let's step out madly and be reckless and dazzling again. Two up, all the way - let's just blaze!

She lifts SHIRLEY to her feet and SHIRLEY walks, tentatively at first… then with the agility of a ballet dancer - as the jukebox strikes up a strain of Rachmaninov.

SHIRLEY   Look at me go!

She pirouettes about. QUEENIE's elated, as if a terrible weight has been lifted from her own being.

QUEENIE   Look at you! Look at you!

SHIRLEY   I can dance, I can fly, I can fall in love all over again…

SHIRLEY dances over to QUEENIE and falls backwards into a 'swoon' - and QUEENIE catches her in her arms.

QUEENIE   Don't do that!

SHIRLEY looks up at her, provocatively.

SHIRLEY   Do what? Risk hurting myself?

QUEENIE   You crazy -

SHIRLEY   Just testing. To see if you'd be there when I needed you…

And QUEENIE pulls SHIRLEY into a romantic kiss, as the lighting state enhances them in radiant Technicolour, leaving OLLIE alone and apart in shadow. The music swells to a finish and they come up for air.

                    Oh my!

QUEENIE   Now we have to be practical.

SHIRLEY   I love you being practical.

QUEENIE   Good. Help me fill out the rest of these to make sure we find each other.

The lighting state reverts as they go to work on their clipboards - and OLLIE turns away and slumps on the banquette.

SHIRLEY turns to look at her, concerned.

SHIRLEY   Ollie? Are you okay?

OLLIE   Nup. I've abandoned all hope now I've re-imagined the worst that awaits. Even alcohol couldn't cheer me up now.

SHIRLEY   Oh please don't say that. I can't bear things to be hopeless.

OLLIE   Well you just carry on being a happy twosome.

SHIRLEY   But we can't be happy if you're sad. That's the way it works, isn't it?

OLLIE ignores.

                    Oh poor Ollie. I think she's really given up.

QUEENIE joins OLLIE.

QUEENIE	Now look, old chap -
OLLIE	Oh don't try and boy talk me. You got the girl. I lost. Story of my lives.
QUEENIE	You'll get another girl.
OLLIE	No ta. I'm going to reincarnate as a dung beetle. Eat shit and be merry.
QUEENIE	Well just leave the paperwork to us.
SHIRLEY	*(Flourishing OLLIE's clipboard)* Tick tick!
QUEENIE	No doubt you'll be a great loss to the insect world, but I think we should return you to your true vocation.
SHIRLEY	And next time Nurse Ollie happens to fall head over heels for a lovely someone - well we won't let you lose her again so be told.
QUEENIE	No more playing the scallywag for you, m'lad.

QUEENIE gives OLLIE a pat on the head - and OLLIE sits up sharply.

OLLIE	Oh what? Are you bloody bonkers? I'm not going back for another round of that.
SHIRLEY	We all have to go back and do better, don't we? So we can move on and upwards.
OLLIE	*(Launching off the banquette)* Well I'm moving sideways. Gimme that clipboard.

OLLIE snatches back her clipboard and pen and makes vigorous scratching out.

	Sod the Sisterhood... *(She ticks the board anew)* There! Sex: Male. Sexuality: Hetero.
SHIRLEY	Oh as if! Don't be silly.
OLLIE	I'm serious. And fuck Dorset, I want some sun... Sorrento. *(Ticking a box)* Stupendo!
SHIRLEY	But you can't just suddenly -
OLLIE	Well I have. So yah-boo-sucks. Queenie said it straight off - got it bang on the button. Who in their right mind, if they had a choice, would tick the dopey double whammy I did last time? Female? Homo? On Planet of the bloody Apes?
SHIRLEY	But that's why we so admire you, Ollie. You didn't take the cowardly way out. You stayed true to yourself no matter what, didn't you?
OLLIE	Booze must've addled my brain then, 'cos the cringe-making memories are coming back thick and fast now. All the ducking and diving, dreading the jokes and the jibes, taking 'sensible precautions' to protect myself... Big butch me daredn't even let a plumber come and fix my boiler, 'less I hid all my knick-knacks and let him

call me 'Mrs'. Well stuff that for another lifetime. I'm not being lumbered with the 'L' for Losers word. I'm joining the red-blooded rat pack, me. I'm going to be a young Romeo on a Vespa, living la dolce vita. Shagging signorinas by the score with my proud Papa's blessing.

SHIRLEY But that wouldn't be *you*, Ollie. You could never be a man - you said - you've got an in-built aversion to male appendages in any form.

OLLIE Well I've got over myself. They can stick an elephant's trunk between my legs if I'm on the right end of it. The bigger the better. *(Looking up, cupping hand to ear)* Any objection upstairs?

No response.

Nup? Well that's me sorted. Swinging dicks rule!

She goes to slap her clipboard on the plinth.

SHIRLEY's shocked. She turns to QUEENIE, who remains rigid.

SHIRLEY Why won't you say anything? Don't you think this is absolutely shocking?

QUEENIE She doesn't mean it.

OLLIE Yes I boop-a-bloody-do. And you soppy dates should wise up too.

SHIRLEY	What - us? *(To QUEENIE)* She thinks we should *all* tick 'Hetero Male'?
OLLIE	Total no-brainer, isn't it? If you want to give yourselves the best shot.
SHIRLEY	But how could we, Ollie? We can't be happy unless we're together. *(To QUEENIE)* We can't, can we?
OLLIE	Well toodle-oo, then. Off you go to la-la on your little lesbo love island in the middle of nowhere. I'm going to lie down and dream of sunny Sorrento. Having my monumental manhood sucked off by a luscious-lipped young signorina. (*She reclines on the banquette and sings*) 'That's amore...'

SHIRLEY turns to QUEENIE, distraught.

SHIRLEY	This is horrible. What's happening? Why would she suddenly give up on us?
OLLIE	Why would I throw in my lot with you two light-weights?
SHIRLEY	But when the Speed Twins come blazing back, we'll be the outest and proudest -
OLLIE	Till you skid off at the next hurdle.
SHIRLEY	But we won't, Ollie, we promise -

QUEENIE   Oh don't rise to her. She's only playing Devil's advocate. Trying to 'test our resolve'.

SHIRLEY   Is she?

QUEENIE   Which I resent.

SHIRLEY   But we've got to make her trust us.

OLLIE   Correcto.

QUEENIE   I'm just waiting for it to dawn on little Romeo he might have to be born a Catholic.

OLLIE   Yeah? Well no probs for me, 'cos I'll be made in the image of God then, won't I? So your call, matey. Roger wilco over and out. And remember the clock's ticking.

She lies back and leaves SHIRLEY and QUEENIE to it.

SHIRLEY   But I don't know what else to say. I've made my choice. I want to stick to it. Otherwise I don't know where I'd start…

She looks at QUEENIE.

             Unless… Are you thinking you want to change - ?

QUEENIE   No. I've learnt my lesson, Shirley. All I want is to be with you and live the life we lost last time.

SHIRLEY   Are you sure?

QUEENIE	Beyond doubt. Come what may.
SHIRLEY	To love and to cherish?
QUEENIE	In sickness and in health.
SHIRLEY	Forsaking all others? Till death us do part?

QUEENIE pulls her into a protective hug.

QUEENIE	Till death has no dominion.

SHIRLEY looks over QUEENIE's shoulder at OLLIE.

SHIRLEY	Do you believe us now, Ollie?

No response.

    She's not answering.

QUEENIE	Just re-tick her boxes.

OLLIE sits up, sharply.

OLLIE	Don't you re-tick my boxes. You haven't said anything to change *my* mind.
SHIRLEY	But we'll never do a wobbly again.
OLLIE	All I heard you promise was to couple up till Kingdom come. Sod all reasons why you want to tick 'Homo Female'.
SHIRLEY	Because that's - because how else?
OLLIE	Not your only option, is it?

SHIRLEY   What do you mean? You don't mean - ?
             (To QUEENIE) Does she mean tick
             'Homo *Male*'?

OLLIE   Who in their right mind wouldn't, if they
             had to tick 'Homo'? Boys' team's still tops.

SHIRLEY   But I couldn't be me at all - if I were a
             boy. I can't even imagine it.

OLLIE   Nah scotch that, pet, too many valuable
             assets to get lost in translation. But if you
             want to be the lovers all the World loves,
             you've still got the obvious option left.

SHIRLEY   What?

OLLIE   You tick 'Female', she ticks 'Male', you
             both tick 'Hetero'.

SHIRLEY   But - she wouldn't want to tick 'Male' any
             more than me.

OLLIE   Why not? She's already owned up to the
             odd crippling wave of penis envy. *(To
             QUEENIE)* So why not bite the bullet
             and go the whole hog, eh? Give the girl a
             proper wedding to look forward to. The
             'socially superior' sort you only get if one
             of you pees standing up.

QUEENIE   You really don't know when to stop, do
             you?

OLLIE   You were the one who couldn't hack it last
             time.

SHIRLEY But Ollie -

OLLIE She knows what I'm on about. *(At QUEENIE)* Look at the drippy Bobby Both-Ways, in her suit with her lippy on. Why don't you butch up and be a real man?

QUEENIE Because then Shirley wouldn't love me, obviously.

OLLIE Wouldn't you, Shirley? If she was still the same person?

SHIRLEY Well yes / but -

OLLIE Exactly. *(To QUEENIE)* Why wouldn't she, eh?

QUEENIE Because I wouldn't *be* the same person, would I?

SHIRLEY Well no / but -

OLLIE Exactly. *(To QUEENIE)* She doesn't want you to be the same wet rag you were last off, does she? All she wants is you to shape up and stand by her, but you're still making her do all the running. So I'm telling you - if you've got an ounce of doubt you can't deliver as a dyke - you'd better stop fannying around and grow a pair of balls.

QUEENIE's silent. SHIRLEY's champing at the bit.

SHIRLEY Um… Excuse me. Can I speak for myself now, please?

OLLIE gives her the floor and lies back down.

(To QUEENIE) Of course if you were a man I'd still love you, if I recognised you as you. And maybe I would fancy you, too, I don't know, but - I didn't try and find a man *like* you the last time. Because what was so exciting was all about us both being girls - being special and different and daring - that's what made it so *sexy*... And it just takes my breath away, imagining how it would be to really live like that - to know other girls and boys like us - to be part of a whole 'scene', with nightclubs and parties… And I know some people will be horrible to us, but we've just got to take that risk and be ourselves. Or nothing means anything, does it?

QUEENIE's silent, distracted. And the light dims down all around her.

Where have you gone? What are you thinking?

QUEENIE I suddenly feel so very old, Shirley... So very old and feeble…

SHIRLEY I can't hear you. Where are you?

QUEENIE   You're so full of energy and courage. Just as you always were. But I feel enmeshed in cobwebs, my lungs full of dust...

SHIRLEY   Oh please come back to me, come back. We've got to convince Ollie we'll stay the course.

QUEENIE looks in OLLIE's direction.

QUEENIE   But she's right...

She looks out.

> It wasn't just the normal world I felt safe from when we were on our little island...

She looks in SHIRLEY's direction.

> I wanted young and beautiful us to be far away from the taint of *her*, Shirley. Her and all her type. As if they were nothing to do with us...

She stares out for a long beat, as if this last admission has drained her.

SHIRLEY   *(Faint)* Say what you're thinking, just say it...

And the lights fade back up as a galvanised QUEENIE stands over OLLIE.

QUEENIE   I want to make you a personal apology.

OLLIE   Do you now?

QUEENIE   For making negative judgements about you based solely on your appearance and demeanour. For using you as a figure of fun to hide my own fear. For spitting on your kindness. For supposing myself superior. For resenting your courage. For ridiculing your / honesty -

OLLIE   Enough, okay.

QUEENIE   Is that enough for you to forgive me?

OLLIE   Oh shut up, will you?

QUEENIE   Get back on your feet and shut up yourself, then. We're in this together. So let's all go back fighting and full of hope.

SHIRLEY   Please, Ollie - you can't jump ship now.

QUEENIE   We want you to be our chum.

She extends a hand to OLLIE.

Beat.

Then OLLIE groans.

OLLIE   I suppose two chums are better than none.

She puts her hand in QUEENIE's and allows herself to be pulled back on to her feet.

SHIRLEY   So can I re-tick your boxes, Ollie?

OLLIE   Go on, then. *(SHIRLEY gets to it)* But they'd better not have banned alcohol in

> our absence or I won't be staying for another menopause.

Then a distant bell starts to toll.

SHIRLEY   Listen!

OLLIE   That'll be the bell for 'Time's up'…

SHIRLEY   Already?

SHIRLEY quickly finishes with OLLIE's clipboard and piles it on the plinth with her own and QUEENIE's.

> There!

The bell tolls louder.

QUEENIE   Don't be scared. All shall be well. And all manner of thing shall be well.

OLLIE   Oh don't over-egg it.

SHIRLEY   We've got to think of all the things we really miss. The good things. Like chocolate…

All are daunted by the bell - as elements of the set start to peel away.

SHIRLEY   Oh come on, quickly, let's think of them. All the good things we miss. That we're going to get back.

OLLIE   Booze and fags.

QUEENIE   Wine and coffee.

SHIRLEY   A nice cup of tea…

Dong. Dong.

QUEENIE   Dogs.

OLLIE   Cats.

SHIRLEY   Horses.

OLLIE   Wild birds…

Dong. Dong.

QUEENIE   Trees.

SHIRLEY   Flowers.

OLLIE   Grass.

SHIRLEY   Picnics!

Dong. Dong.

QUEENIE   Riding a motorbike.

SHIRLEY   A Speed Twin!

OLLIE   Driving a vintage sports car. Preferably a 1961 Aston Martin DB4.

SHIRLEY   You can't. That's pollution.

OLLIE   So's an old motorbike.

QUEENIE   Both converted to run on bioethynol…

Dong. Dong.

                Healthy things… Playing tennis.

SHIRLEY   Swimming.

OLLIE   Pass.

SHIRLEY	Going for a walk.
QUEENIE	In the rain.
SHIRLEY	By the seaside.
QUEENIE	Over the downs.
SHIRLEY	Down the dales.
QUEENIE	Through the forest.
OLLIE	To find a delightful restaurant…

Dong. Dong.

SHIRLEY	Hide and seek! 'Cos we've got to think of childish things, too, now.
QUEENIE	Childish things…
OLLIE	Oh god…
SHIRLEY	Oh come on!

The bell tolls louder still. They all have to shout above it.

OLLIE	Jelly and ice cream!
QUEENIE	Skipping!
SHIRLEY	Sand castles!
OLLIE	Jam doughnuts!
QUEENIE	Tobogganing!
SHIRLEY	Snowballs!
OLLIE	Toasted marshmallows!

Dong. Dong.

SHIRLEY	Some new things. That we've never done before. Like - going to university!
OLLIE	Snorting cocaine!
QUEENIE	Having lesbian sex!

SHIRLEY swoons, taken by surprise.

SHIRLEY	Oh my god! I just felt that whoosh again…

Dong. Dong.

QUEENIE	Oh just say anything…
OLLIE	Art!
QUEENIE	Books!
OLLIE	Telly!
SHIRLEY	Cuddly toy.
OLLIE	What?
SHIRLEY	Sorry, I'm all flustered now…

Dong. Dong.

OLLIE	Oh bloody hell…
QUEENIE	*(Arm round SHIRLEY)* Going to the theatre!
SHIRLEY	Ballet!
OLLIE	Cricket!
QUEENIE	Running a business!

SHIRLEY   Making a home!

OLLIE   Sleeping!

QUEENIE   Awakening!

Dong. Dong.

SHIRLEY   Having children!

QUEENIE looks at her, taken aback.

QUEENIE   Children?

SHIRLEY   Our children. We can have children.

QUEENIE   Having children!

They both look to OLLIE.

OLLIE   Being their favourite Auntie!

The bell sounds one last echoing dong.

SHIRLEY   There's loads to look forward to…

OLLIE   Yup…

SHIRLEY   It's just so scary -

She chokes, hand to mouth, suddenly overwhelmed by the enormity ahead.

            Sorry, but…

OLLIE   I find I really do miss cats…

Chokes, overwhelmed.

QUEENIE   Come on, chums, chin up…

She pulls them into a hug. They hold fast, together, awaiting they know not what, as the lights dim down all around them. Then the jukebox lights up.

> Look! We can have a last dance before we go. My choice now.

She goes to the jukebox, fishing in her trouser pocket for change.

> Here we are...

She presses buttons, then draws herself up tall and defiant.

> Let's bloody well go for it!

The jukebox blasts out 'The Locomotion' by Little Eva. As loud as possible.

QUEENIE goes for it, dancing over towards the others, as if teaching them the moves anew.

Then they dance in a line-up.

Then QUEENIE comes to the fore, as OLLIE and SHIRLEY peel away and disappear.

QUEENIE's left dancing alone, giving it everything.

Then the music cuts out, searingly - and QUEENIE is frozen in her last pose - as if shocked still - eyes staring.

Blackout.

Over the blackout we hear the distorted soundscape of bleeps, buzzers, heartbeats and laboured breathing fading back up.

Shadowy figures dressed as hospital orderlies come and go, briskly.

We anticipate the scene of a birth.

The lights go up on the set transformed into:

Nurses' station in a private hospice, London.

ANGELICA, late thirties, smartly suited, sits alone in the waiting area.

She's been waiting for some time, but too tense and distracted to read a magazine.

Then a uniformed SENIOR NURSE enters, carrying a clipboard and a cardboard box to the nurses' station. She has short grey hair and a brisk demeanour, but she seems troubled.

ANGELICA stands.

ANGELICA   Sister?

The NURSE looks up, surprised to see her.

NURSE   Miss Angelica? You can't still be here?

ANGELICA   I came back. Didn't they tell you?

NURSE   Tssk. My bleep must be on the blink.

ANGELICA   I wondered if there was any development? Roberta McQueen? I've got to go back to Dorset tonight. Has she given you any message at all for my mum Shirley?

NURSE   I'm sorry, m'dear.

ANGELICA   Well couldn't you please just let me see her, just for five minutes? I know that's why Mum's been holding on.

NURSE	I'm afraid our Queenie passed away. Over an hour ago. She had a sudden heart attack.
ANGELICA	Oh no.
NURSE	Just like that.
ANGELICA	Oh no.
NURSE	I should've been with her. I promised her. But I got called away to another patient.
ANGELICA	She had a heart attack?
NURSE	She didn't say another word after I gave her that photograph of her and your mum. Well only when she cried out about her little dog. Tufty. Thought he was about to get run over. 'Though he's been dead ten years himself, she told me before.
ANGELICA	She didn't say anything about Mum?
NURSE	I tried to get through to her. Believe me, pet, I told her my jokes, I told her all sorts - anything to help her make her peace. 'Cos seeing the priest didn't help, I can tell you that. She was convinced she had more time than she did.

ANGELICA's upset.

ANGELICA	I'm sorry. I really so hoped…
NURSE	She was a difficult old stick, but I was sad to lose her. I mean we've all got baggage,

but… *(Sighs)* Got to try and trace her own daughter now, hand these things over. There was obviously a big rift there… But here's your photo, look. *(Fishes it out of the box and hands it over)* Not much else she had with her. Bible. Rosary beads. Makeup.

ANGELICA   If - when you find her daughter, would you please give her my card? Would you say I've got some information for her about our mothers, she might want to know?

She hands over a business card. The Nurse pockets it.

NURSE   Okey-dokes. Do my best.

ANGELICA   Thank you. She's my only link now…

ANGELICA stares at the photo, dabbing her eyes.

Then the NURSE's bleep suddenly goes off. She withdraws it from her pocket.

NURSE   Well-halle-finally…

She switches it off, in deference to ANGELICA's focus.

It's a smashing photo. Look a proper pair of head-turners, didn't they?

ANGELICA   They called themselves 'The Speed Twins'. They meant everything to each other once. It's so sad…

The NURSE is frowning.

NURSE   What's that smudge on it? Is that lipstick?

ANGELICA   My eyes are swimming.

The NURSE takes back the photo, tilts it to the light, peers at it.

NURSE   That's a lipstick kiss...

ANGELICA   Is it?

NURSE   Look, there - on your mum's face. That's a lipstick kiss.

ANGELICA   She kissed it?

NURSE   She kissed your mum's face.

ANGELICA takes the photo back and looks at it anew. And could cry with joy.

Blackout.

The End.